Implementing Web-Scale Discovery Services

Practical Guides for Librarians

About the Series

This innovative series written and edited for librarians by librarians provides authoritative, practical information and guidance on a wide spectrum of library processes and operations.

Books in the series are focused, describing practical and innovative solutions to a problem facing today's librarian and delivering step-by-step guidance for planning, creating, implementing, managing, and evaluating a wide range of services and programs.

The books are aimed at beginning and intermediate librarians needing basic instruction/guidance in a specific subject and at experienced librarians who need to gain knowledge in a new area or guidance in implementing a new program/service.

About the Series Editor

The **Practical Guides for Librarians** series was conceived by and is edited by M. Sandra Wood, MLS, MBA, AHIP, FMLA, Librarian Emerita, Penn State University Libraries.

M. Sandra Wood was a librarian at the George T. Harrell Library, The Milton S. Hershey Medical Center, College of Medicine, Pennsylvania State University, Hershey, PA, for over 35 years, specializing in reference, educational, and database services. Ms. Wood worked for several years as a Development Editor for Neal-Schuman Publishers.

Ms. Wood received a MLS from Indiana University and a MBA from the University of Maryland. She is a Fellow of the Medical Library Association and served as a member of MLA's Board of Directors from 1991 to 1995. Ms. Wood is founding and current editor of *Medical Reference Services Quarterly*, now in its 35th volume. She also was founding editor of the *Journal of Consumer Health on the Internet* and the *Journal of Electronic Resources in Medical Libraries* and served as editor/co-editor of both journals through 2011.

Titles in the Series

1. *How to Teach: A Practical Guide for Librarians* by Beverley E. Crane
2. *Implementing an Inclusive Staffing Model for Today's Reference Services* by Julia K. Nims, Paula Storm, and Robert Stevens
3. *Managing Digital Audiovisual Resources: A Practical Guide for Librarians* by Matthew C. Mariner
4. *Outsourcing Technology: A Practical Guide for Librarians* by Robin Hastings
5. *Making the Library Accessible for All: A Practical Guide for Librarians by* Jane Vincent
6. *Discovering and Using Historical Geographical Resources on the Web: A Practical Guide for Librarians* by Eva H. Dodsworth and L. W. Laliberté
7. *Digitization and Digital Archiving: A Practical Guide for Librarians* by Elizabeth R. Leggett
8. *Makerspaces: A Practical Guide for Librarians* by John J. Burke
9. *Implementing Web-Scale Discovery Services: A Practical Guide for Librarians* by JoLinda Thompson

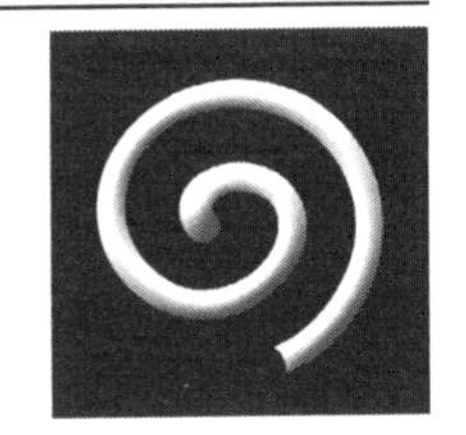

Implementing Web-Scale Discovery Services

A Practical Guide for Librarians

JoLinda Thompson

PRACTICAL GUIDES FOR LIBRARIANS, No. 9

ROWMAN & LITTLEFIELD

Lanham • Boulder • New York • London

Published by Rowman & Littlefield
A wholly owned subsidiary of The Rowman & Littlefield Publishing Group, Inc.
4501 Forbes Boulevard, Suite 200, Lanham, Maryland 20706
www.rowman.com

16 Carlisle Street, London W1D 3BT, United Kingdom

British Library Cataloguing in Publication Information Available

Library of Congress Cataloging-in-Publication Data
Thompson, JoLinda.
Implementing web-scale discovery services : a practical guide for librarians / JoLinda Thompson.
pages cm. — (Practical guides for librarians ; no. 9)
Includes bibliographical references and index.
ISBN 978-0-8108-9126-5 (pbk. : alk. paper) — ISBN 978-0-8108-9127-2 (ebook : alk. paper) 1. Online library catalogs. 2. Online bibliographic searching. 3. Federated searching. 4. Library Web sites. 5. Library catalogs and users. 6. User interfaces (Computer systems) 7. Libraries—Special collections—Electronic information resources. I. Title.
Z699.35.C38T48 2014
025.04—dc23 2014017072

∞™ The paper used in this publication meets the minimum requirements of American National Standard for Information Sciences—Permanence of Paper for Printed Library Materials, ANSI/NISO Z39.48-1992.

Printed in the United States of America

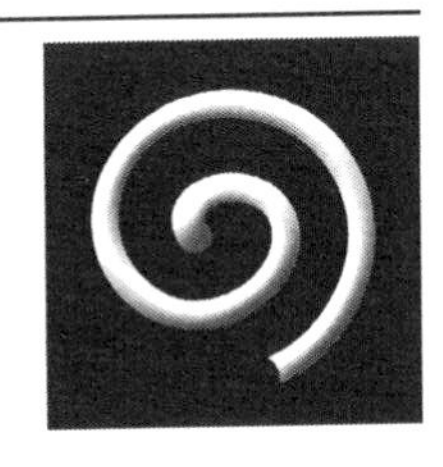

Contents

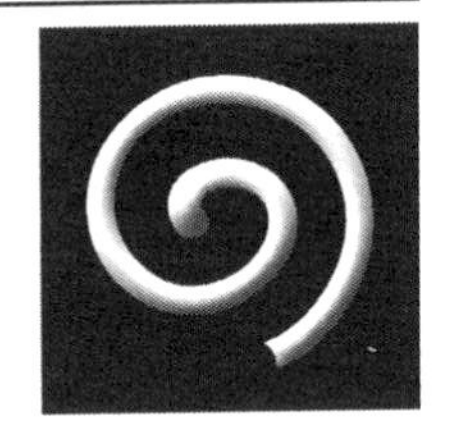

List of Figures and Table

Figures

Table

Preface

Since 2009, web-scale discovery services have emerged as the answer to Google for many libraries wanting to provide a quality, one-search service that can provide users quick and easy access to the full spectrum of their resources. These services were initially implemented in academic libraries, and many college and university libraries have since moved toward adopting them. Public library systems, secondary schools, and special libraries are now increasingly considering web-scale discovery as a service for their users.

Boston College High School's library is an example of this next group of libraries to adopt web-scale discovery. The head librarian, Tia Esposito, reports an enthusiastic reception from students there and says that initial resistance from libraries in their consortiums and collaboratives has given way to interest in also subscribing.

For this second wave of libraries considering web-scale discovery, the selection and implementation process can be daunting. The number of products available, their complex nature, and the expense of implementation make adoption a major undertaking. Extensive investigation and planning are required to purchase, configure, and launch a web-scale discovery service.

The purpose of *Implementing Web-Scale Discovery Services: A Practical Guide* is to inform prospective purchasers about what specifically they are considering buying and to aid them in evaluation, purchase, and implementation. It does not recommend specific services. Instead, it gives potential subscribers the tools to make an informed decision to select the best product for their users and collections, and it shares tips for optimizing the service for their specific environment.

"The Evolution of Web-Scale Discovery in Libraries" (chapter 1) provides background on the development of these systems, discussing how they emerged over time to address the shortcomings of federated search and next-generation catalogs in the quest to present users with a viable alternative to Google. This chapter also defines exactly what web-scale discovery is and what distinguishes it from other discovery products. Chapter 2, "A Closer Look at Web-Scale Discovery Options," profiles in detail the four web-scale discovery products currently on the market, examining such factors as what content each draws on, what discovery layer functions are available (e.g., facet configuration and record presentation), and what special features distinguish them from the competition (including social media and recommender services). Alternatives to web-scale discovery are also discussed.

Subsequent chapters address each phase of a selection project, identifying decision points and questions to ask prospective vendors, which will help move the project forward in an orderly and focused manner. It shares the experiences of many libraries that have launched a service and published or presented about it. Chapter 3, "Making the Best Content Match for Your Library," gives practical tips for identifying the audience for web-scale discovery and how to identify the system with the best content match to meet its needs. Chapter 4, "Evaluating the Discovery Layer," looks at the search interface and features available for narrowing and managing search results. Chapter 5 considers other important features and functions, including mobile interfaces, API, and usage statistics generation. Each chapter includes a list of questions to address within the library or with vendors to evaluate prospective products.

The steps involved in selecting a tool are addressed in chapter 6—from assembling the right team to evaluate and select to implementing trials and negotiating price. Once a system has been purchased, all libraries will need to work through making the optimal content available for users, which is detailed in chapter 7, and tailoring the discovery layer for local needs, addressed in chapter 8. All three of these chapters include lists of tasks to work through, and chapter 6 has a tool for comparing several products head-to-head and scoring them.

When a service is finally ready to be launched, there is additional work, including marketing campaigns, figuring out where to place search boxes and widgets to reach the most users, and presenting the web-scale discovery service in a way that communicates what it is and how it fits in with the library's other search and discovery tools. Instruction is another important and often overlooked and underestimated part of a web-scale discovery implementation project. Tips for what to teach and how to reach users at point of need are included in chapter 9.

To optimize a service for the library environment, usability testing can aid in detecting problems with configuration and identifying search interface features that need further refinement. Chapter 10 looks at usability testing in detail, providing a step-by-step guide for planning a usability test and an analysis of previously published usability tests of web-scale discovery services.

These services are complex and interlinked with many of a library's other systems and processes. Chapter 11 examines maintenance issues, ranging from day-to-day system administration to getting the most out of usage statistics and the impacts to collection development, document delivery, and cataloging services.

In the past three years, web-scale discovery services have evolved and developed substantially, and more change is on the horizon. In chapter 12, some of the problems challenging web-scale discovery, including the content wars, are addressed. One of the solutions, the movement toward standards for these systems, is considered with other emerging trends, such as further personalization of search and the potential impact of linked data and altmetrics.

Implementing Web-Scale Discovery Services attempts to include the very latest information available, but it is hard to capture a moving target. While the book was in final manuscript preparation, OCLC announced the imminent transition of WorldCat Local to WorldCat Discovery Service, and Serials Solutions announced the demise of the company name and separate identity within ProQuest. Chapter 11 includes resources, publications, and social media tools for keeping up with changes to the library resource discovery market.

Web-scale discovery services are complex, and there are many considerations for libraries that are prospective purchasers. This book should help even those new to library discovery to have the tools to launch a successful selection and implementation process. The result may be a decision to add just a discovery layer (e.g., Bibliocommons), or enhanced content, such as book jackets, tagging, and reviews to the existing OPAC. Or, as with Boston College High School, web-scale discovery could be put in place for electronic content, with the goal to add catalog records later. Whatever path a library decides to take, *Implementing Web-Scale Discovery Services* will provide important information and guidance toward reaching the goal of improved access to content, collections, and services for users.

Acknowledgments

Authoring this book was by far the biggest writing project I have taken on in my career.

There are many people to thank for their assistance in gathering information, helping me present it in an organized and coherent manner, and generally supporting me during the process.

First, I thank the editing team at Scarecrow Press—in particular, Sandy Wood, who was the frontline editor. Her experience and constructive criticism were invaluable, as were her eagle eyes. Sandy had the tedious job of finding and fixing all the grammatical and punctuation errors and suggesting more intelligible ways to explain things. She also was a huge help in pointing out where a figure or sidebar might be appropriate or how a chapter's content might be better organized. I also thank Charles Harmon and Robert Hayunga for entrusting me with this important and timely title in their series of Practical Guides books.

As I gathered information, I contacted all the major vendors for information about their products. I further thank Kathy McEvoy at EBSCO Information Services for her prompt and diligent response to all of my requests and to EBSCO for kindly allowing use of a number of images. Bob Murphy at OCLC had the challenge of providing me with this information as WorldCat Local was transitioning to WorldCat Discovery Service. Luckily, he was able to get me important information about this change as I was completing the manuscript, and OCLC allowed use of several images. Thanks also to Scott Schuetz and Christine Goetz for information on Summon and allowing use of images from Oregon State University Libraries' Summon service and to Ex Libris for allowing use of images from Northwestern University Library's Primo service. And thanks to the following libraries who agreed to usage of images from their services and websites: Montana State University Library, Northwestern University Library, Oregon State University Libraries, Queens College Library, University of Georgia Libraries, and University of Washington Libraries.

Tia Esposito, head librarian at Boston College High School, very graciously agreed to share her firsthand experiences with implementing web-scale discovery in a secondary school setting. As very little has been written about web-scale discovery implementations outside of academic settings, this was a valuable perspective to include in the book. I thank her for her time and input.

My coworkers at Himmelfarb Health Sciences Library also played a role in preparing me for writing the book and supporting me during the writing process. Laura Abate and Kathe Obrig served with me on Himmelfarb's Discovery Task Force, and the three of us had many conversations, wrapping our minds around the concept of web-scale discovery, what it would mean for library users, and if it was the right choice for the library. The experience implementing a system at Himmelfarb provided the background and a framework for what librarians need to know and do to put a service in place. It was an invaluable learning process. I also thank my colleagues Steve Brown and Chris Cook for keeping an eye out for relevant literature as I was writing this and Andy Puro in document delivery for getting items in my hands quickly.

Many individuals have shared their experiences selecting and implementing web-scale discovery services in academic libraries in particular. There is already a substantial amount of information available to read, digest, and learn from, and sometimes I feel like I just scraped the surface in pulling this book together. Thanks to those who have written and presented extensively in this area—particularly, Jason Vaughan, Marshall Breeding, Athena Hoeppner, and Doug Way.

Last but not least, I thank my family and friends—especially my husband, Rob, and daughter, Kerrie—for their support during this effort, which took me away from them for long periods for more than a year. I am grateful for their patience and encouragement when I needed it.

CHAPTER 1

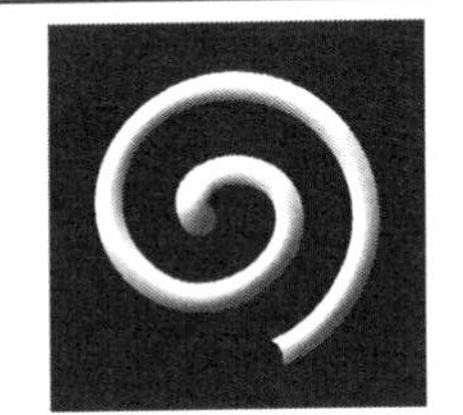

The Evolution of Web-Scale Discovery in Libraries

IN THIS CHAPTER

- ▷ Tracing the Origins of Web-Scale Discovery
- ▷ Defining Web-Scale Discovery

Tracing the Origins of Web-Scale Discovery

IN THE FIRST DECADE OF THE TWENTY-FIRST CENTURY, the game changed for libraries. At workstations in homes, offices, and schools, people were increasingly turning to Google and other web-based search engines for their information-seeking needs. Google was easy to get to and use. All that was required was a browser and Internet connection, and the world of information on the Internet was at the inquirer's call via a simple keyword search. So pervasive was the phenomenon that the verb *googling* gained an entry in the *Merriam-Webster Dictionary* by 2006 (Keizer 2006): "to use the Google search engine to obtain information . . . on the World Wide Web" (*Merriam-Webster* 2012).

The vast quantity of information available via Google expanded exponentially by middecade. Google Scholar was introduced in 2005, making the full-text archives of scholarly publishers available for searching (Cochran 2005). By 2009, 2,900 publishers were participating, including IEEE and ACM (Jacsó 2010). Google Books was launched in 2004, originally as a partnership project with publishers, but a new partnership with five research libraries included the goal of scanning much of the material on their shelves (Ojala 2006). Though these projects were fraught with technical and legal challenges, their result put much of the world's literature and published research at the fingertips of the average Google searcher.

With more searchers turning to Google and more content increasingly available through Google, the library world started to turn its attention to the threat of being marginalized by this new world of search and discovery. In the 1990s, the online public access catalog revolutionized how library users found materials in library collections. By the late 1990s, many of these online public catalogs (OPACs) were in web-friendly form, but the search access points and even the display of records were quite similar to what was available in the old card catalog. Library users were now used to the ease of searching Google, the plethora of graphics on most webpages, and the sample book pages, reviews, and social media features on Amazon and Barnes and Noble's websites. The average library online catalog had swiftly diminishing appeal by comparison.

At the same time, libraries were ramping up the number of materials available electronically. University students and faculty in academic libraries, as well as patrons of major public library systems, were often faced with a dizzying array of databases available for searching. Packages of electronic resources made large volumes of subscription content available to users in these settings. In an attempt to organize and make these electronic collections accessible to users, libraries created A–Z lists of sources and subject guides. But these services were often rejected or ignored by users who found it easier to just "google it."

Recognition of the library world's failure to deliver easy and comprehensive access to rapidly growing collections of electronic resources available to users was being discussed and written about midway through the 2000–2010 period. In 2005, OCLC commissioned Harris Interactive to administer a survey to learn more about people's information-seeking behavior and the value of the library "brand." The study findings were a wake-up call:

> The findings presented in this report do not surprise, they confirm. During the hundreds of *Scan* discussions and meetings held over the past 24 months, several recurring themes surfaced. "Users are not aware of the electronic resources libraries make freely available." Our survey findings bear this out. "Users are as comfortable using Web information sources as library sources." Our study shows this perception also to be true, across countries, across U.S. age groups, across library card holders and non-card holders. "The library brand is dated." Again, our survey findings do not surprise, they confirm. (OCLC 2005, 11)

The OCLC survey found that 55% of users completely agreed that Google provided worthwhile information versus 33% for their library's website. Factors that tipped in favor of Google and other search engines included speed, convenience, and ease of use. Of those surveyed, 58% were unsure if their library offered electronic resources, and reported monthly usage of online databases and electronic materials was less than 25%. Overwhelmingly, survey respondents most closely associated the library "brand" with books.

A year later, the Library of Congress released a report called for by the LC Bicentennial Conference on Bibliographic Control titled *The Changing Nature of the Catalog and Its Integration with Other Discovery Tools*. The project was led by Karen Calhoun (2006), then of Cornell University Library, and the publication became known in the library community as the Calhoun report. In the introductory section, she writes,

> Today, a large and growing number of students and scholars routinely bypass library catalogs in favor of other discovery tools, and the catalog represents a shrinking proportion of the universe of scholarly information. The catalog is in decline, its processes and structures are unsustainable, and change needs to be swift. (5)

The Calhoun report was controversial because it called for streamlining library processes and greatly simplifying bibliographic control, positions not popular with some members of the library community. But the action plan at the end of the report also recommended the following to improve the users' experience with the catalog (Calhoun 2006, 19):

- Enrich the catalog with services (e.g., "more like this" and "get it" options, new booklists), and data (cover art, reviews, TOCs).
- Enable much better browsing and organization of large retrieval sets.
- Facilitate best-match retrieval (no search dead ends).
- Provide relevancy ranking of search results.
- Continue working with available technologies (but look for better ones) to federate discovery and delivery of books, journals, and journal articles.
- Link the user to full text whenever possible.

Many of these items were being developed and made available in new systems that were starting to be adopted by the library community to address the challenges of twenty-first-century search and discovery. In his widely read editorial from 2005, "My Kingdom for an OPAC," Andrew Pace featured three of the new products that would become early entries to the "next-generation OPAC" market: Aquabrowser, Red Light Green, and Endeca Profind. Pace cited their relevancy ranking and clustered display features as transformative for the library OPAC. A year later, his institution, North Carolina State University Library, released its customized Endeca Profind instance, taking its catalog into the next-gen OPAC world ("NCSU Libraries" 2006).

Profind was developed primarily for e-commerce, and its meta-relational indexing was used by commercial websites (IBM, Barnes and Noble, Wal-mart) to allow consumers to refine searches for products by price, model, or specification. These same features were now introduced to the library catalog in the form of what would be referred to by vendors as "faceting" or "clustering" of results. In the next-gen OPAC, facets often included categories such as material types, location in the library, subject headings, and publication dates. Users could refine results by using a facet to limit their results to a particular type of material (e.g., books only) or records that had a particular subject heading assigned. Endeca also employed relevancy-ranking algorithms to pull the most relevant records to the top of search retrieval instead of the old OPAC defaults of alphabetical order or order of acquisition.

Endeca Profind got a lot of attention, but it was never widely installed in libraries. Each application was custom, requiring individualized interface design and relevancy-ranking formulas. Pricing and the labor involved in this type of project may have played a factor in holding it back from widespread adoption in libraries. Instead, Aquabrowser became the product most frequently identified with the next-gen OPAC label. Aquabrowser was developed by Medialab and was successful in Europe before coming to the states in a deal with The Library Corporation (TLC). It also utilized relevancy-ranking formulas to pull the best results to the top of hit lists, and it faceted results to narrow by format, author, subject heading, and publication date. Aquabrowser's unique feature was the visual word cloud that displayed the user's search term in the middle of a cloud of associated subject headings, authorities, and keywords generated from the catalog metadata. Users could click on one of the associated terms to refine a search (Ekkel and Kaizer 2007).

By 2009, Aquabrowser was in hundreds of libraries, and traditional library software vendors and open-source developers had competing next-gen OPAC products on the market. These included Encore from Innovative Interfaces, Primo from Ex Libris, World-Cat Local from OCLC, VuFind developed as open source at Villanova University, and Blacklight, another open-source project, developed at the University of Virginia. Marshall Breeding—author of the Library Technology Guides website, an essential source of information for many in the library systems industry—closely followed the development of next-gen OPACs and wrote a summary issue about them in *Library Technology Reports* in 2007 and a book about them in 2010. According to Breeding (2007), these products have the following features in common:

- Faceted navigation
- Keyword searching
- Relevancy ranking
- "Did you mean?" suggestions to correct spelling mistakes
- Recommendations
- Enriched content (cover art images, table of contents, summaries)
- Web 2.0 features, such as tagging and user reviews
- RSS

Breeding also wrote about the need to bring electronic full-text content into these interfaces to make them a true one-stop search option for library users. The integration of federated search technologies into these systems was beginning to make this possible.

Federated search was developed to provide simplified and centralized access for all the new electronic content that libraries were acquiring. Access to this content was frequently "siloed" by a myriad of competing database products and online interfaces, resulting in user frustration and confusion with all the options on library webpages. Federated search, also known as metasearch or broadcast searching, utilizes communications standards (most frequently, Z39.50) to translate a single search query across multiple search platforms. Federated search products—including Metalib (Ex Libris), 360 Search (Serials Solutions), and Webfeat (Webfeat)—came on the market in 2003 and 2004, allowing

TEXTBOX 1.1.

WEB-SCALE DISCOVERY EVOLUTION TIMELINE

2003: Federated search allows multiple databases and catalogs to be searched simultaneously (Webfeat, Metalib, 360 Search).

2005: "Next-generation" catalogs with discovery layer features emerge (Endeca Profind and Aquabrowser).

2007: WorldCat Local delivers the first marriage of discovery layer with central index content (from WorldCat and FirstSearch).

2009: Summon joins the discovery layer with robust "web-scale" central index content.

libraries to purchase a search tool that would allow searching of many databases simultaneously. Most OPAC products are Z39.50 compliant, making it possible for libraries to include the catalog data along with electronic database content.

Federated search was a leap forward, but it had its limitations. It was often slow to retrieve items across all the databases. Database subscriptions that had a low number of concurrent users allowed could frequently be tied up by federated searching if a library was not careful in its selection of resources to include. Vendors developed connectors to databases and electronic resources in high demand, but libraries with specialized collections often had to pay to have connectors built for their more unusual databases and electronic content sources. If a database changed its structure or interface, the related connector would break, and the database would no longer be available until the connector was updated. Of most concern was that federated search tools by their nature demanded a dumbing down of search queries to allow them to work across all the disparate search interfaces and database structures (Boss and Nelson 2005).

In 2009, Serials Solutions (now ProQuest) announced a new search service that would bring the discovery layer technology developed in next-gen OPACs to improve the search experience together with a vast centralized index of electronic content. The product was called Summon. Josh Hadro (2009) of *Library Journal* announced,

> With Summon, a "unified discovery service," Serials Solutions has set its sights on the holy grail of library resource interfaces: a true one-box search, collecting article-level results from electronic resources with local catalog holdings into a single integrated results list. (17)

What was radically different about Summon was the preindexing of content from multiple sources. Instead of connecting to disparate sources, all the content was in one central "normalized" index. At the ALA Midwinter meeting in Denver where Summon was presented to the library world, Mike Eisenberg, former dean of the Information School at the University of Washington, said, "This is the dream. The competition is not other libraries; the competition is Google" (Hadro 2009, 17). The age of web-scale discovery had begun.

Defining Web-Scale Discovery

Web-scale discovery (WSD) systems bring the discovery layer technology developed to improve the search experience in next-gen OPACs and federated search systems together with a large, centralized index of content. This structure allows web-scale discovery to be more efficient and effective than federated search, and it provides a search experience capable of competing with Google and other commercial web search engines in terms of both scope and convenience.

The term *web scale* was used by Amazon and Google to describe the capacity and reach of their cloud computing and search platforms, as noted by Lorcam Dempsey (2007). In these contexts, it was meant to describe how these applications could adjust in scale as they grew larger and larger thanks to the new architectures of the web. The term is now being adopted by library vendors to describe emerging cloud-based services. OCLC and ProQuest have embraced web scale as their approach to offering discovery and resource management services.

According to Marshall Breeding, web-scale systems share the following four characteristics (Breeding 2012, 19):

- Large-scale technology platforms
- Applications delivered through multitenant software as a service
- Massively aggregated approaches to data
- Highly cooperative arrangements among participating libraries

Not only does *web scale* mean "large," but it also equates to the ability to continue to expand without limit. The scope of these systems demand that they be hosted in the cloud, and WSD systems are almost exclusively offered as hosted or cloud-based services. The subscriber does not house the service on local servers.

This ability to host large-scale volumes of content on an ever-expanding platform was necessary to address the shortcomings of federated search. *Multitenant* refers to the fact that multiple libraries are accessing a common data source in the form of a central index of content. Vendors such as Serials Solutions (now ProQuest) realized that putting all the content into a normalized, central index would solve a lot of problems. For one, it makes searching much faster and more efficient to not have to connect to multiple databases and aggregators to retrieve the content. It also eliminates the need to develop multiple connectors to translate the search across all these different interfaces. One index means that the metadata is mapped the same way across all the data sources, making relevancy ranking and faceting more accurate. It can also accommodate more sophisticated search querying and make basic keyword searching more effective.

Web-scale discovery is defined by large centralized indexes of content that are searched through a single search interface. The vendor establishes a base index made up of content from partner publishers and aggregators, which is accessible to all subscribers. Source content frequently also includes open-access data sources, such as Hathi Trust and PubMed. The individual library adds its unique local content (catalog data, institutional repository data, etc.) to the index through a loading process, which usually requires regular updates. The vendor takes the content provided by publishers, open-access sources, and the local library and preharvests the metadata to a normalized central index. For libraries that have a need to include databases or other content sources critical to their users that are not included in the WSD already, connectors can be established, usually for an additional fee. This concept is illustrated in figure 1.1.

Creating the normalized index may involve stripping out and simplifying the original source metadata to optimize it for searching and relevancy ranking across all the disparate content sources in the WSD system. A more thorough discussion of content sources and how they are included and indexed is in chapter 3, "Making the Best Content Match for Your Library."

Central Index Common Features

- Article- and item-level data is provided by publisher and aggregator partners.
- Additional data sources often include open-access sources.
- Local data specific to the library can be included, including catalog data, institutional repository data, and digitized collections.
- Connectors can be established to important databases or other content sources that the WSD does not currently include.

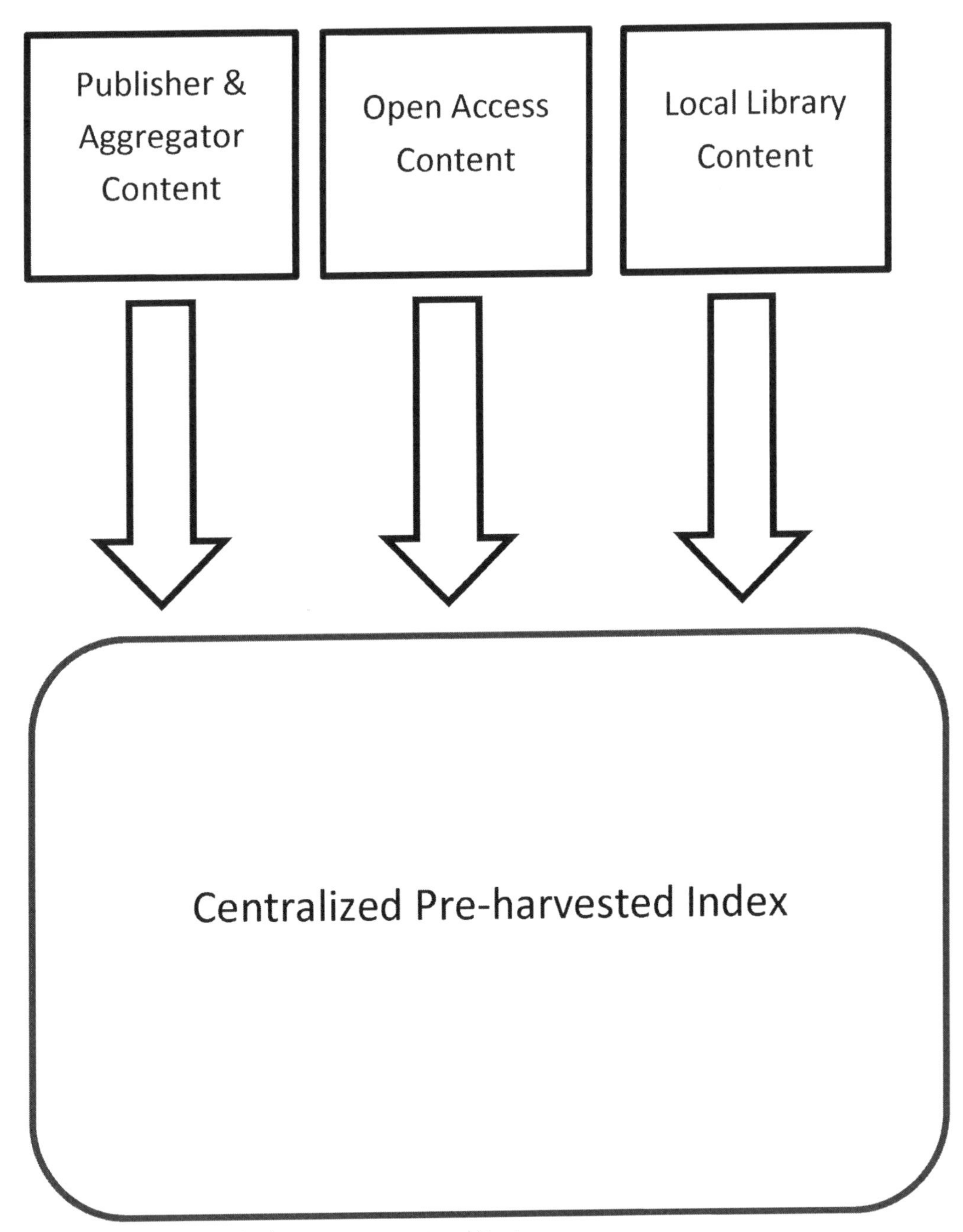

Figure 1.1. Web-scale discovery content architecture.

- Metadata from all the sources is preharvested and normalized to create the library's unique index for searching.

Sitting on top of the content and providing the search interface is the discovery layer. The discovery layer allows searchers to easily navigate the system in an environment that feels familiar to them since it includes many elements from web search engines and retail sites (e.g., Amazon). These common elements include a single search box, relevancy ranking, faceting options to limit retrieval, and easy access to full text.

Libraries can typically opt to offer a single search box that defaults to the keyword index, or it can put an advanced-search option up front with more visible index and limiting selections and the ability to enter multiple search terms with Boolean logic. The search box is frequently developed as a widget that can be embedded on the library's homepage, putting the WSD system front and center as the key discovery tool for users. Further discussion of widget configuration is in chapter 8, "Configuring and Branding the Discovery Layer."

Due to the massive volumes of content that the user typically searches in a WSD system, relevancy ranking is necessary to bring the best results as close to the top of the results list as possible. Most vendors closely guard their relevancy-ranking algorithms (or formulas), as their effectiveness is critical to the success of the service, much as relevancy ranking in web search engines such as Google and Bing are critical to their success. Some services will allow libraries to help refine the algorithm by requesting that local catalog content or other categories of content be boosted in search results.

Searches on a WSD system frequently retrieve thousands of hits, so the ability to refine results is essential. Along with traditional limiting options that users and librarians are used to in advanced-search features of their favorite databases, the discovery layers provide "faceting" or "clustering" features. Facets are usually presented prominently in the left-hand column of the search results page. Faceting categories are derived from the record metadata and present the searcher with options to limit results by fields available

TEXTBOX 1.2.

WEB-SCALE DISCOVERY GLOSSARY

Web-Scale Discovery: "A pre-harvested central index coupled with a richly featured discovery layer that provides a single search across a library's local, open access, and subscription collections" (Hoeppner 2012).

Discovery Layer: The user interface and search system for discovering, displaying, and interacting with the content in library systems, such as a web-scale discovery central index.

Central Index: "A collection of content that is systematically harvested from diverse sources such as journal publishers, database producers, library catalogs and collections, open source full text, repositories, etc. The harvested content is then processed and pre-indexed to facilitate quick searching" (National Federation of Advanced Information Services 2013).

Facet: Categories derived from content metadata that provide the searcher with options to quickly narrow search results. A subject facet allows the searcher to limit search results to just records assigned a particular subject index term.

Relevancy Ranking: "The program used by a search engine to rank search results and display them in order of decreasing relevance based upon a set of predefined factors" (National Federation of Advanced Information Services 2013).

in the records. For example, typical faceting options include the ability to limit results by subject heading, material type, content provider, and publication date. Facets can be more specialized in applications where there is a focus on more specific subject-oriented content sources. Facet options could also include geography, industry codes, subject age for research data sources, and so on.

In the relatively rare instance where the search retrieves few results, many systems have spell-check and "Did you mean?" features built in to aid the searcher. The WSD system will look for commonly occurring metadata terms and phrases that are the closest match to the user's query and suggest these as possible search terms. The most effective of these will automatically pop up an option to search the more common derivative of what the searcher put into the search box and will show results with the suggested term.

The search result hit list presents brief records for items retrieved. Most systems offer some de-duping features so that identical items retrieved from multiple sources are removed. Some products provide record merging to centralize the record data from multiple sources into one super record. The number of records displayed per page can typically be configured by the library, as well as what aspects of the brief record it wants to display up front to the user. Abstract and even image previews from the records can often be included. Many systems automatically bring in jacket art to make results more visually appealing to searchers. For content that is mutually licensed by both the library and the web-scale discovery vendor, links directly to full-text content can be included in the brief record. For other subscribed content, the WSD system provides a link to the library's link resolver, which supplies options for obtaining the full text or document delivery options. Records that come from the local catalog can be configured to display the current location and status of the item (available, checked out).

WSD systems also deliver sophisticated record management tools, including links to bibliographic management services such as RefWorks and EndNote, social media sites such as delicious and Reddit, and RSS feeds. Searchers can typically create a permalink to a record or a search strategy, generate a citation on the fly, download a bibliography of search results, or e-mail search results. Other common social media features include the ability to tag and review records on some systems. These are usually an opt-in feature that the subscribing library can control.

Common Features of Discovery Layers

- Relevancy ranking of results
- Faceting or clustering features that enable refinement of retrieval by common metadata fields (subject, location, publication date)
- "Did you mean?" search suggestion or spell-checking features
- De-duplication features to eliminate duplicate result records
- Direct links to full-text content
- Record management features for results, including citation generation, e-mailing or downloading of results lists, or creation of permalinks and RSS feeds
- Links to social media sites and bibliographic management tools (EndNote)
- Optional Web 2.0 features, including user reviews and tags

Discovery layers provide one-box searching, navigation tools, easy access to full-text content, and a front end to the preharvested central index of WSD services. The addition of the discovery layer is illustrated in figure 1.2.

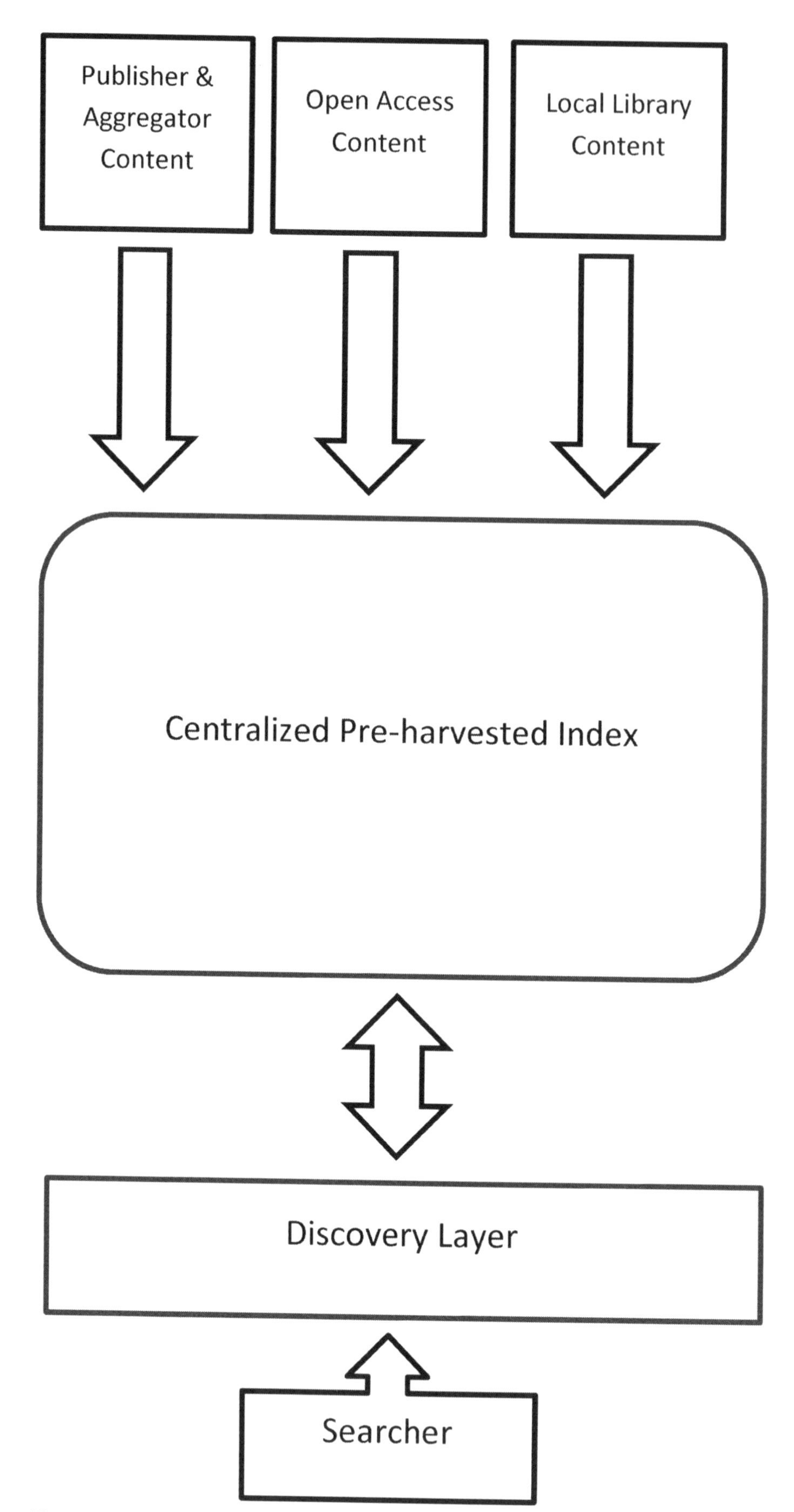

Figure 1.2. Web-scale discovery content and discovery layer architecture.

Web-scale discovery has the potential to deliver a system that is as convenient and familiar as a web search engine while providing users with access to much of the library's trusted content through one search interface. For libraries, these systems offer the ability to control and tailor the content and to brand and optimize the discovery layer to best meet their users' needs. Their potential is great, but their nature is complex. As such, librarians need to carefully comparison shop the WSD systems available to identify the product that is a best match to local needs. Chapter 2 discusses the products currently on the market.

Key Points

Web-scale discovery products, which first came to market in 2009, are distinguished by a large central index of bibliographic, article-level, and full-text content. Content is obtained directly from publishers and aggregators via partnership agreements and brought in from open-access sources such as HathiTrust and Google Books. This content is combined with local content from the subscribing library, including catalog and institutional repository records. These records typically need to be uploaded to the service on a regular basis. This marriage of local bibliographic content with article-level full-text content (subscription based) allows libraries to provide an efficient and comprehensive one-search system to library users.

WSD systems feature a user-friendly discovery layer, which provides a simple one-box search input for keyword searching. Relevance-ranking algorithms sort retrieval, filtering the most relevant results to the top of the hit list. Facets allow searchers to drill down to the most desired results by limiting by material type, publication year, content source, or other indexes. Integration of link resolvers allows easy linking to full-text when available through the library's current subscriptions. Tools to manage retrieval frequently include citation generation, export to RefWorks or social networking sites, saving to lists, e-mailing results, or setting up RSS feeds. The combination of discovery layer functionality with a massive cloud-based centralized and normalized index of content defines web-scale discovery.

TEXTBOX 1.3.

RECOMMENDED FURTHER READING

Breeding, Marshall. 2012 "Library Web-Scale." *Computers in Libraries* 32, no. 1: 19–21.

Hoeppner, Athena. 2012. "The Ins and Outs of Evaluating Web Scale Discovery Services." *Computers in Libraries* 32, no. 3: 7–10, 38–40.

Luther, Judy, and Maureen C. Kelly. 2011. "The Next Generation of Discovery." *Library Journal* 136, no. 5: 66–71.

All three of these articles provide an excellent summary of the concepts of web-scale discovery services in libraries.

References

Boss, Stephen C., and Michael L. Nelson. 2005. "Federated Search Tools." *Reference Librarian* 44:91–92.

Breeding, Marshall. 2007. "Next Generation Library Catalogs: Introduction." *Library Technology Reports* 43, no. 4: 5–14.

———. 2010. *Next-Gen Library Catalogs*. New York: Schuman.

———. 2012 "Library Web-Scale." *Computers in Libraries* 32, no. 1: 19–21.

Calhoun, Karen. 2006. *The Changing Nature of the Catalog and Its Integration with Other Discovery Tools: Final Report*. Washington, DC: Library of Congress. http://www.loc.gov/catdir/calhoun-report-final.pdf.

Cochran, Shannon. 2005. "Google Scholar Launched." *Dr. Dobb's Journal* 30, no. 2: 14.

Dempsey, Lorcam. 2007. "Web Scale." *Lorcam Dempsey's Web Log*. Blog. January 5.

Ekkel, Taco, and Jasper Kaizer. 2007. "AquaBrowser: Search and Information Discovery for Libraries." *Information Services and Use* 27:79–83.

Hadro, Josh. 2009. "Summon Aims at One-Box Discovery." *Library Journal* 134, no. 3: 17–18.

Hoeppner, Athena. 2012. "The Ins and Outs of Evaluating Web Scale Discovery Services." *Computers in Libraries* 32, no. 3: 7–10, 38–40.

Jacsó, Péter. 2010. "Metadata Mega Mess in Google Scholar." *Online Information Review* 34, no. 1: 175–91.

Keizer, Gregg. 2006. "'Googling' Lands in Dictionary." *Information Week*. July 7. http://www.informationweek.com/googling-lands-in-dictionary/190300949#.

Merriam-Webster. 2012. "Googling." http://www.merriam-webster.com/dictionary/googling.

National Federation of Advanced Information Services. 2013. *Recommended Practices: Discovery Services*. Philadelphia, PA: National Federation of Advanced Information Services. http://info.nfais.org/info/Recommended_Practices_Final_Aug_2013.pdf.

"NCSU Libraries Release Endeca-Powered Facetted Catalog." 2006. *Library Hi Tech News* 23, no. 2: 27.

OCLC. 2005. *Perceptions of Libraries and Information Resources: A Report to the OCLC Membership*. Dublin, OH: OCLC. http://www.oclc.org/en-US/reports/2005perceptions.html.

Ojala, Marydee. 2006. "Reviewing Google Book Search." *Online* 30, no. 2: 12–14.

Pace, Andrew. 2005. "My Kingdom for an OPAC." *American Libraries* 36, no. 2: 48–49.

CHAPTER 2

A Closer Look at Web-Scale Discovery Options

IN THIS CHAPTER

▷ Profiling Web-Scale Discovery Services Currently Available

▷ Examining Discovery Layer–Web-Scale Content Hybrids

▷ Exploring Web-Scale Discovery Alternatives

Profiling Web-Scale Discovery Services Currently Available

THE FOLLOWING INCLUDES A PROFILE AND EXAMINATION of the features of currently available web-scale discovery (WSD) services. This is a rapidly growing marketplace, and the systems are constantly evolving; as such, this information is subject to change, and other products may be available by the time of publication. Links to the product information for each system and recent publications are included in the profiles. Note that all vendors were contacted for the most current information, but not all responded. Therefore, the following information was taken mostly from previously published information, the vendor's websites, and observation of implemented sites where the author had access.

Web-Scale Discovery Services Profiled

- EBSCO Discovery Service, EBSCO Publishing
- Primo, Ex Libris
- Summon, ProQuest
- WorldCat Discovery Service (formerly WorldCat Local), OCLC

Profiles include the following:

- Product overview and brief history
- Central index content

- Integration of local and catalog content
- Relevancy ranking and metadata
- Retrieval display, refinement, and management features
- Social media, recommender, and special content features
- API, customization, and mobile features
- Platform and purchasing options
- Recent publications

EBSCO Discovery Service, EBSCO Publishing

Product Overview and Brief History

EBSCO released its entry to the WSD market, EBSCO Discovery Service (EDS), in January 2010 in the wake of Serials Solution's (now ProQuest) vaunted release of Summon in early 2009. EBSCO representatives explain that the extra year of development was used to "deliver better breadth and depth of coverage and a powerful platform with better built-in customization" (Brynko 2011). Once EDS got to the market, the two systems became fierce competitors, culminating in a showdown at the annual Charleston Conference on book and serial acquisitions in fall of 2010 where representatives of both companies pitched their vying products in a face-to-face session (Rapp 2010). EDS and Summon became the early heavyweights on the market, helped by their parent companies' positions as serials and content management vendors. Like ProQuest, EBSCO had an established pool of content and relationships with content providers to draw from in creating an extensive base index.

EBSCO had experience developing discovery services as a database provider, and libraries that already receive many of their databases and full-text content through EBSCO*host* will find advantages in using EDS. The discovery layer has a similar look and includes many features available through other EBSCO*host* database products.

Central Index Content

EDS claims to offer the most comprehensive list of information providers of any of the discovery services (EBSCO 2012). At end of 2012, EBSCO reported content from 20,000 partner providers and metadata from another 70,000 publishers, including JSTOR, Thompson Reuters, ABC-CLIO, LexisNexis, and Newsbank. EDS draws largely from EBSCO's EBSCO*host* service, which hosts 350 databases, 300,000 e-books, and tens of thousands of full-text journals and magazines. Access to EBSCO-purchased e-texts or e-journals is enhanced by one-click link to PDF and HTML full text in the search results list, known as SmartLinks (see figure 2.1). EDS works with all link resolvers to provide full-text access to sources that are not subscribed directly through EBSCO.

Integration of Local and Catalog Content

Libraries that purchase EDS will need to regularly load catalog records and other local collections that they want to include in the base index. Update of catalog records can be as frequent as daily. Catalog configuration and Z39.50 connections to the library's ILS enables EDS to pull in live status and location information for display in catalog records. These records can be enhanced with jacket art and data from sources such as Google Books. Libraries can opt to enable composite book records that use FRBR (Functional

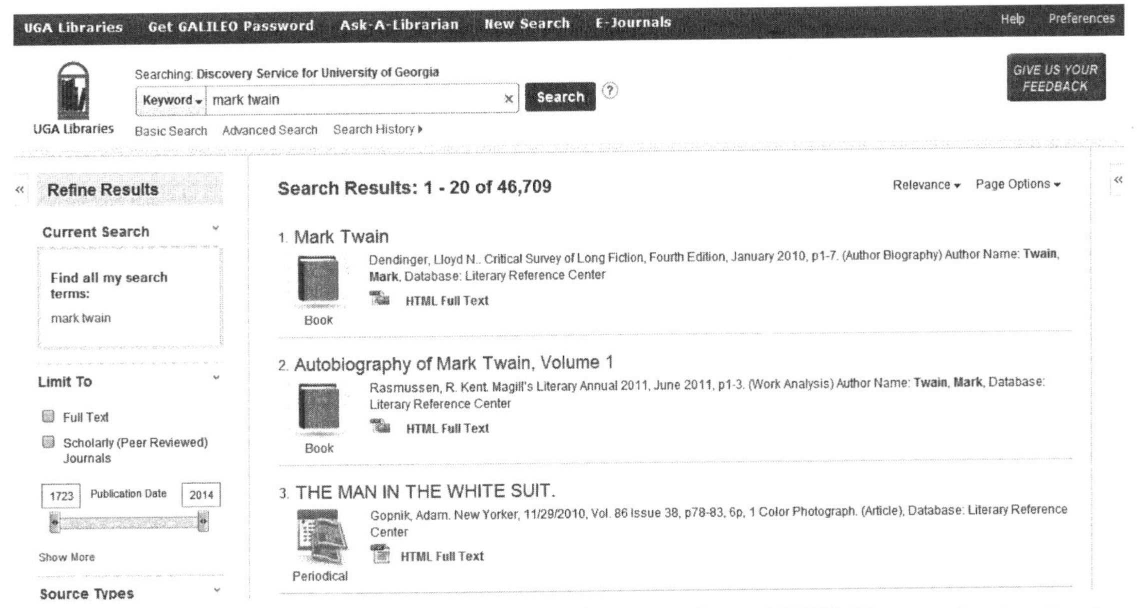

Figure 2.1. Search for Mark Twain on the University of Georgia Libraries' EBSCO Discovery Service. *Courtesy University of Georgia Libraries, University of Georgia, Athens, GA.*

Requirements for Bibliographic Records) to consolidate information about various formats and editions of a work. Local repository records can be loaded in any XML format that is OAI-PMH retrievable, including Dublin Core, EAD, METS, and MODS.

EDS offers features to accommodate consortia customers. Catalog sharing for all libraries that are EDS customers displays the home library's holdings for catalog records and provides union catalog holdings information for the other customer libraries. Links to ILL requesting can be included in the full record for catalog records.

Relevancy Ranking and Metadata

In marketing EDS, EBSCO puts emphasis on its relevancy-ranking algorithms and its ability to draw from the subject indexing available on EBSCOhost. EDS's relevancy ranking favors subject heading and controlled vocabulary fields over hits in the abstract and full-text content when this metadata is available. Along with also weighting exact matches and density (frequency of match), EDS adds factors such as currency, document type, and length of the item retrieved (research articles are usually longer than newspaper articles). Libraries can also opt to more heavily weight local catalog records in relevancy ranking.

EDS exploits the more comprehensive indexing and metadata of many native sources on EBSCO*host* by creating connectors to search on that data directly. EBSCO insists that this is not federated searching, but the indexing and metadata exist outside the EDS base index.

Retrieval Display, Refinement, and Management Features

EDS presents search retrieval in a two- or three-column page that can be customized. The left column includes limiters and facet groups. The limiters presented at the top of the column include options for limiting to full-text and peer review articles, by publication date, or by source type. Facets are derived from the metadata fields in the central index and additional database sources. They usually include language, subject, publication, and content provider but can also include more specialized fields from the content sources (i.e., geography or industry codes).

The middle column contains the results list, which outputs in relevancy rank order. It can be optionally sorted by date using the pull-down menu at the top. Libraries can determine the default brief record display, and users can use the pull-down menu options to include more or fewer fields and adjust number of results per page. As mentioned earlier, if full-text content is available through an EBSCO source, an HTML or PDF link will appear in the brief records for easy click-through to the content. If not, the library can configure a link to the local link resolver to appear here. Another pull-down menu at the top of the middle column allows users to add results to a folder and create alerts or permalinks to the search.

An optional third column can include a chat help window to the library's IM reference tool, connectors to content sources not included in the central index if enabled (labeled "Integrated Resources" by default), and previews of image and video content from retrieved records. Full record view also provides access to an extensive list of tools to save, bookmark, export, and create permalinks to the record (see figure 2.2). The citation feature allows users to generate a bibliographic citation for the record in a variety of citation formats, including APA and MLA. Users can opt to create accounts that allow them to permanently save results lists and search strategies.

Social Media, Recommender, and Special Content Features

Libraries that have critical databases or sources not included in the central index or currently available through EBSCO can opt to develop connectors to those sources as "integrated search" targets for a fee. The connector will use federated search to retrieve records and interfile them with the regular EDS sources.

EBSCO recently introduced Research Starters for EDS, described as a "fully citable placard feature." They give the searcher a quick, encyclopedia entry–like overview of a topic and can be configured to appear in search results, when searchers enter 50,000 commonly used search terms. Data for the Research Starters come from reference e-texts (Salem Press Encyclopedias are a common source) and provide links to related topics.

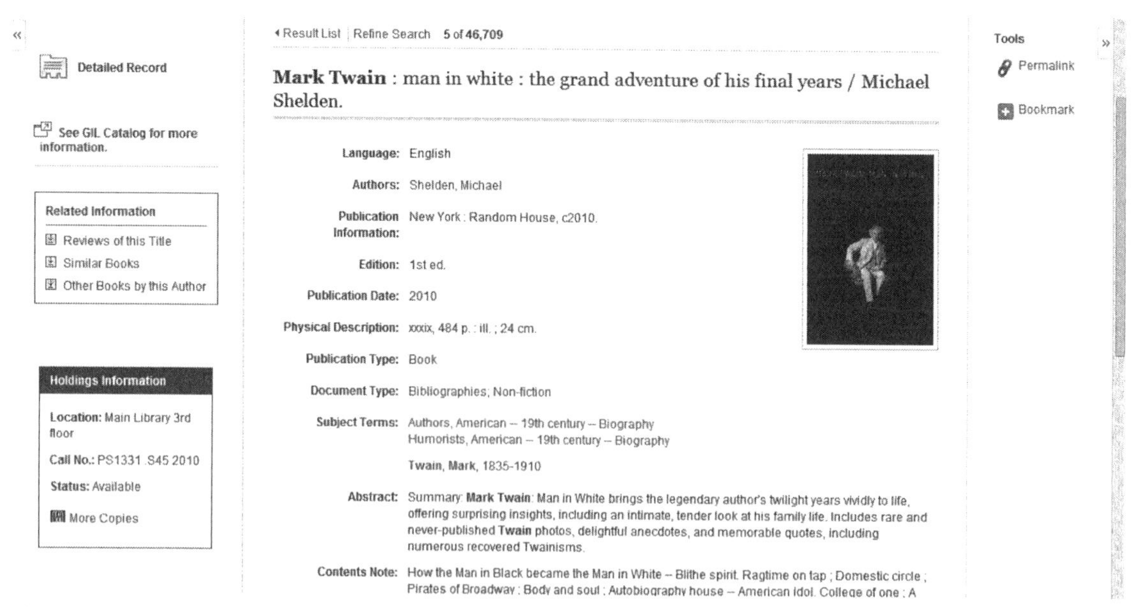

Figure 2.2. Full record display from the University of Georgia Libraries' EBSCO Discovery Service. *Courtesy University of Georgia Libraries, University of Georgia, Athens, GA.*

EDS does not have recommender or native social media services, but libraries can integrate third-party services such as ChiliFresh (http://www.chilifresh.com) or GoodReads (https://www.goodreads.com) to provide review and tagging services. Libraries can also opt to configure widgets to provide direct link to additional content about records from a variety of sources, including LibGuides, GoodReads, RSS Feeds, Flickr, Wikipedia, and so on. Widgets can be displayed in search results brief view, full record view, or both.

API, Customization, and Mobile Features

EBSCO recently released an API (application programming interface) for EDS. The API allows libraries to integrate EDS content with other services, such as an institutional repository, learning management systems such as Moodle, web front end, or even another discovery layer service (see section "Examining Discovery Layer–Web-Scale Content Hybrids"). These tools are available to all EDS customers, and EBSCO provides detailed documentation for programmers. For consortia customers, each library can build a profile to accommodate the subject needs of its users and can individually brand its space. This ability to build specialized profiles and branding is available for single library customers as well, allowing a library to create spaces for individual departments or groups with more specific needs.

EDS Mobile optimizes search and display on most mobile platforms, including iPhone/iPod, Android, and BlackBerry. Apps are available for iPhone/iPod and Android. iPads connecting to EDS function in the regular full desktop mode.

Platform and Purchasing Options

EDS is offered exclusively as a cloud-based service hosted by EBSCO. There is no option to purchase and host it on local servers. The company has also recently entered into agreements with ILS and discovery layer providers (Innovative, SirsiDynix, OCLC) to supply EDS content through these interfaces. See the section in this chapter on hybrid systems for further information.

EBSCO provides an administrative interface that allows customers to easily change branding and search interface settings, facet groups, and content sources available. Statistics reporting is also available via this administrative module, which is the same as that supplied for EBSCO*host*.

EBSCO reports 5,612 EDS installations worldwide in February 2014. Pricing is typically by annual subscription, based on FTE and level of service (factoring how many local content sources and connectors need to be configured). Discounts are available for consortial implementations and multiyear subscriptions. Free trials are available for prospective customers. More information about EDS is available at http://www.ebscohost.com/discovery/.

Recent publications about EDS include the following:

Brynko, Barbara. 2011. "EDS: A Single Point of Discovery." *Information Today* 28, no. 3: 33.

Thompson, JoLinda, Kathe Obrig, and Laura Abate. 2013. "Web-Scale Discovery in an Academic Health Sciences Library: Development and Implementation of the EBSCO Discovery Service." *Medical Reference Services Quarterly* 32, no. 1: 26–41.

Vaughan, Jason. 2011. "EBSCO Discovery Services." *Library Technology Reports* 47, no. 1: 30–38.

Williams, Sarah C., and Anita K. Foster. 2011. "Promise Fulfilled? An EBSCO Discovery Service Usability Study." *Journal of Web Librarianship* 5, no. 3: 179–98.

Primo, Ex Libris

Product Overview and Brief History

Primo was first released in 2007 as a next-generation catalog product. Though it came from an ILS vendor (Ex Libris sells and supports the Aleph, Voyager, and Alma ILS products), it was developed to serve as an enhanced catalog product for any ILS product, like its next-gen OPAC competitors. Libraries that purchased Primo offered patrons a single search interface for their catalog records and other local collections.

Ex Libris had the vision to see the potential for web-scale discovery early on, and unlike its traditional ILS vendor competitors, it developed a product that could go head-to-head with EDS, Summon, and WorldCat Local. A central index of full-text, article-level content called Primo Central was developed in 2010. The combination of the Primo discovery layer and Primo Central content is a true web-scale discovery system. Its next-gen catalog origin provides a rich and fully developed discovery layer. Throughout the book, references to Primo should be understood to be the combination of the Primo discovery layer and the Primo Central content.

Central Index Content

When Primo Central came to market, it had 300 million items from publishers, aggregators, and open-access sources, and that central index has grown as Ex Libris continues to enter into partnerships to remain competitive with the other WSD systems. Content providers include Thomson-Reuters, LexisNexis, Gale, and ebrary (see figure 2.3). Ex Libris recently announced a deal with Elsevier to make its popular sci-tech-medical database, Scopus, and associated content available for searching in Primo. Ex Libris and EBSCO have reached an impasse over inclusion of EBSCO*host* content in the Primo Central index. See further discussion of this in chapter 12 (in the "Moving toward a More Equitable Content Environment" section).

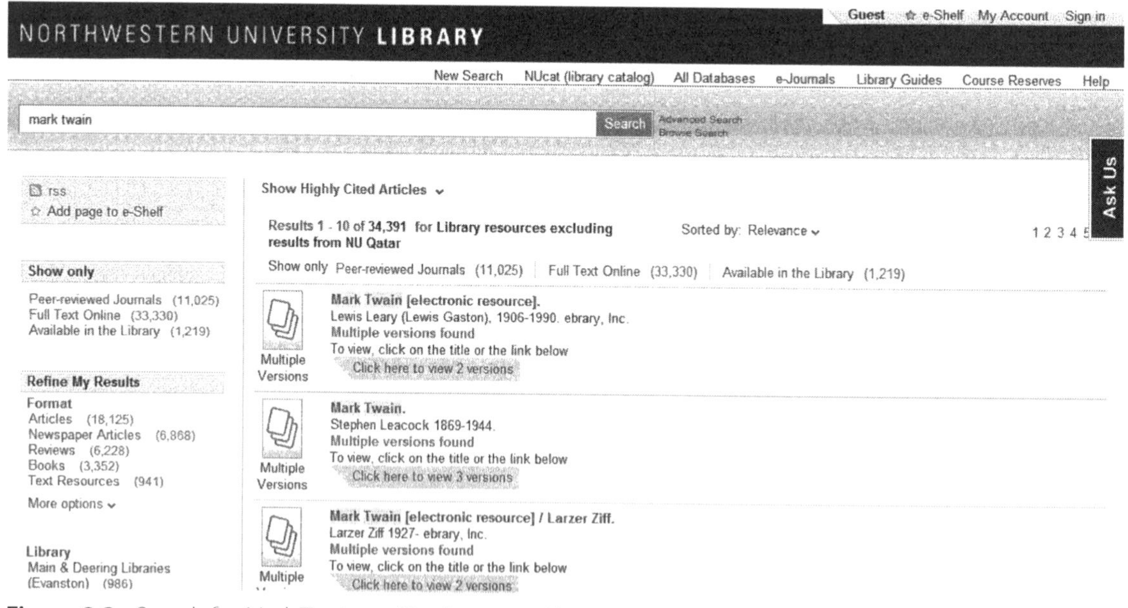

Figure 2.3. Search for Mark Twain on Northwestern University Library's Primo Service. *Courtesy Northwestern University Library, Northwestern University, Evanston, IL.*

Integration of Local and Catalog Content

Primo marries its central index content with the local content that subscriber libraries supply. For libraries that are customers of Aleph, Voyager, and now Alma (Ex Libris's new resource management system), processes are scheduled to run regularly to load new records and update ILS records. Libraries on other ILS products will need to configure and schedule regular catalog feeds (which can be as frequent as daily) to get local data into the system. Primo accommodates many diverse data standards (MARC, Dublin Core, XML) and delivery methods, allowing inclusion of records from systems such as Fedora, Digital Commons, dSpace, and ArchivalWare. Primo then "normalizes" harvested content into a Primo record format (Vaughan 2011a).

Relevancy Ranking and Metadata

Primo's relevancy ranking formula takes into account a number of factors, such as frequency of term match in a record, currency, and the number of times that a record was previously accessed. It also allows field weighting, called "boosting," that can be controlled and configured by the subscriber library. Libraries can select to boost individual items to promote them in searches. Local catalog materials are automatically boosted through a service called "blending," which prevents local content from being overwhelmed by article level metadata.

Primo recently introduced Scholar Rank to improve relevancy ranking. Scholar Rank uses an item value score derived from the bxArticle recommender (detailed below) and the number of times that an item is cited in the literature, user characteristics (dependent on the user logging in and developing a profile on the system), and information needs (determined by search semantics). For example, a simple search query such as "global warming" implies that the user is looking for broad general materials, while a more detailed query indicates a need for greater specificity.

Retrieval Display, Refinement, and Management Features

Search results are presented in relevance ranked order, but a pull-down menu allows users to change the sort if desired. Duplicate records are grouped, with the publisher record preferred for display when it exists in the system. Faceting options are displayed to the left, which include predefined facets common across all systems. As with many other features of this system, customers can choose to develop their own unique facet groups.

Records from the local catalog system can also be highly tailored in their display. Customers can determine what elements of the catalog item record are retrieved to indicate item location and current status. If the library subscribes to a content-enrichment service, jacket art enhances the records. Records without jacket art are identified with a standard record type icon (see figure 2.4). Links to external services that provide additional content, such as Amazon or WorldCat, can be configured. For article full-text and electronic results, libraries can configure any link resolver to deliver full text and can customize what links to additional content are presented.

Primo also provides a variety of ways to export and save search queries and results, including RSS feeds, export to bibliographic management services such as EndNote and RefWorks, and an e-Shelf option. The e-Shelf acts like a shopping cart in a web commerce site, allowing users to save results for later reference. Users who log in can save

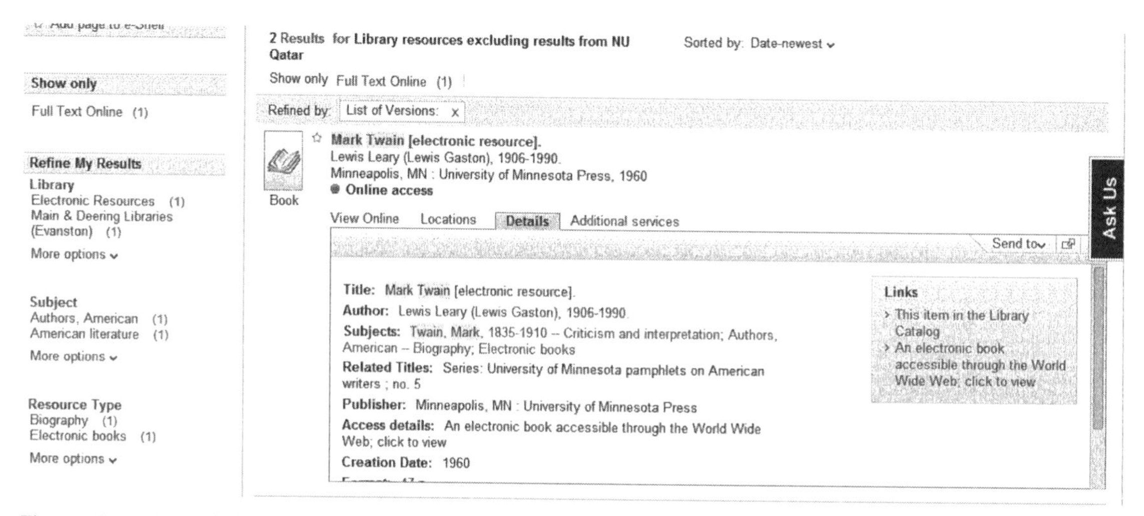

Figure 2.4. Record display detail on Northwestern University Library's Primo Service. *Courtesy Northwestern University Library, Northwestern University, Evanston, IL.*

their e-Shelf content indefinitely, while those who do not can keep the e-Shelf active only during their search session.

Social Media, Recommender, and Special Content Features

Primo has a fully integrated user tagging, rating, and review service. These can be librarian-mediated if desired. Users are required to log in to use these services and other user services features, such as requests, renewals, and retrieval of holds and fine information.

Unique to Primo is the bxArticle recommender service. This service pulls data derived from Ex Libris's Open URL link resolver service, SFX. Libraries that are SFX subscribers can opt to have their usage data contributed and analyzed to make connections between records. When a user executes a search on a Primo system that has the bx recommender service enabled, a window of recommended results appears in the search results list based on what other users who viewed those same results also viewed and retrieved.

API, Customization, and Mobile Features

Primo allows a high degree of customization for libraries with the resources to devote to creating a unique, tailored search interface for users. An API layer and web services allow for anything from standard branding and matching the look and feel of the customer's existing web presence to a complete reconfiguration of the search screen or export of content to other search interfaces. The APIs are well documented through the Ex Libris's EL Commons portal. Libraries can also set up multiple tailored portals to serve particular user groups or individual libraries within a consortium. A standard template featuring a single search box configuration is available for the customer that prefers something more out of the box.

Other features of Primo include comprehensive consortia options, multilingual support (including CJK), access from mobile devices, and an administrative interface that provides access to statistical data, including top searches with no results and facet usage (Luther and Kelly 2011).

Platform and Purchasing Options

The Primo Central index content is in the cloud; however, the Primo discovery layer software can be purchased as a hosted service or for local installation. Ex Libris offers three levels of support for Primo—Local, Directed, and Total Care. These differ by how much the subscriber wants to take care of locally (hosting and configuration) with Total Care, including cloud hosting and comprehensive support. Because the configuration and pricing models can vary, libraries should contact Ex Libris for further information. In his 2014 LTR article, Breeding reports Primo in approximately 1,900 libraries. Installations are in a variety of library types, including academic, special, government, and public libraries, although the majority of installations are at academic institutions. More information about Primo and Primo Central is available at http://www.exlibrisgroup.com/category/PrimoOverview.

Recent publications about Primo include the following:

Baumann, M. 2010a. "Ex Libris' Primo Continues Expansion." *Computers in Libraries* 30, no. 4: 39.

———. 2010b. "Ex Libris Releases Primo Central." *Computers in Libraries* 30, no. 7: 42.

Poulter, Dale. 2012. "Primo Central: A Step Closer to Library Electronic Resource Discovery." In *Planning and Implementing Resource Discovery Tools in Academic Libraries*, edited by Mary Pagliero Popp and Diane Dallis, 535–43. Hershey, PA: IGI Global.

Vaughan, Jason. 2011. "Ex Libris Primo Central." *Library Technology Reports* 47, no. 1: 39–47.

Summon, ProQuest

Product Overview and Brief History

Summon came onto the market with a bang in early 2009. The product announcement was made at the ALA Midwinter meeting that January, and reviews from bloggers and library journalists attending the meeting were glowing:

> My killer-app moment was with Summon, a new unified-search service from Serial Solutions that does what we really want a product like this to do: natively indexes data from its sources (databases, e-books, OPACs, etc.) so that retrieval is fast and consistent. Summon makes your typical metasearch tool look like a rusty wagon with square wheels. (Schneider 2009)

> With Summon, a "unified discovery service," Serials Solutions has set its sights on the holy grail of library resource interfaces: a true one-box search, collecting article-level results from electronic resources with local catalog holdings into a single integrated results list. (Hadro 2009)

Though WorldCat Local was available over a year previous, Summon received the attention and the press of being an all new type of product. This may have been due to the scale of Summon. Right off the bat, Serials Solutions (now ProQuest) had content partnerships with more than thirty major publishers, including Gale, Nature Publishing Group, Oxford University Press, and ProQuest. This translated to a central index of more than 300 million items representing 50,000 journal titles (Breeding 2009).

At the time of its product announcement, Summon was in beta at two major U.S. academic libraries: Dartmouth and Oklahoma State University. Dartmouth released an evaluation document at the end of the beta period in fall 2009. Undergraduate students were enthusiastic about Summon, but graduate students preferred subject-specific databases. Overall, Dartmouth librarians expected that Summon would replace WebFeat (their federated search tool) and that it addressed a need for a convenient "large scale discovery tool" (Dartmouth College Library 2009). Summon became established as the best known of the WSD products early on.

Central Index Content

Like all the WSD products, Summon has evolved considerably over the past three years and has continued to add a steady stream of content partnerships. ProQuest promotes the transparency of its content coverage. Lists of key databases, participating publishers, and serial titles included can be viewed from the ProQuest website at http://www.serialssolutions.com/en/services/summon/content-and-coverage. All prospective customers receive a complimentary analysis of journal title holdings against those in the Summon central index. In November 2012, Serials Solutions (now ProQuest) announced an initiative to increase the e-book presence in Summon by adding indexing and availability of full-text of 400,000 titles from HathiTrust and ebrary.

Integration of Local and Catalog Content

Libraries will need to load local records that they want to regularly include in the central index. There is considerable flexibility in the types of records that can be included. MARC, Dublin Core, XML, and EAD are all acceptable, and ProQuest will work with libraries to import records from homegrown systems that do not adhere to a data standards schema. Summon allows libraries to share their local digital and repository records with the Summon community at large if desired, which provides a large pool of these records from academic systems throughout the world for subscriber libraries.

In fall of 2012, Summon added opportunities to include enhanced content from Syndetics Solutions (http://proquest.syndetics.com) or Library Thing (https://www.librarything.com/forlibraries) to catalog records, including jacket art, table of contents, and ratings and reviews. Linking options for placing holds or submitting document delivery requests can also be configured (Peterson-Sloss 2012). The added content and services can enhance the catalog records brought into Summon by the subscriber library and are the first steps in providing the functionality needed for a library to outright replace its OPAC with Summon.

Relevancy Ranking and Metadata

Standard installation delivers a single keyword search box with an option to link to an advanced search interface with more options for Boolean search and limits. Keyword searching is across metadata and full text of the source records. Summon's relevancy ranking tailors the algorithm to the record type and weights metadata in particular fields higher than others. Additional weighting is given to peer review data sources for journal literature and currency. For full-text matching, frequency of term use and proximity of search terms are used. Summon's exact algorithm is proprietary and being constantly refined, like the other WSD systems.

Retrieval Display, Refinement, and Management Features

Summon has a range of facet options that display on the left side of the search results screen to refine retrieval, including several filters that allow users to quickly limit to or eliminate particular types of content. A full-text filter allows searchers to easily limit to just full-text results. Similarly, a news filter allows users to quickly eliminate newspaper content if desired, and libraries can opt to enable this filter by default. A scholarship filter limits to just peer review journal literature.

Brief records in the search results screen typically include item location (for catalog records), resource type, and full-text availability. The full record displays as a pop-up window when the brief record title is hovered over (see figure 2.5). Duplicate records are merged and enhanced with outside sources, including Ulrich's and Serials Solution's journal authority data. Searchers can also easily create an RSS feed based on the current search for regular updates.

Summon relies on the local URL resolver software to direct users to full text, frequently with one click. If full text is available via ProQuest, a suite of features for displaying and saving the citation and full-text article is offered. Searchers can generate formatted citations in common bibliographic styles with the click of a button to cut and paste into other applications, or they can export citations directly to RefWorks or EndNote. Full text can be saved in a variety of formats, including HTML and PDF.

Social Media, Recommender, and Special Content Features

Results can be posted to social media sites such as Facebook or Twitter or e-mailed to other recipients. A "More Like This" button in the full record display screen offers related records that the searcher can link to directly. A unique feature of Summon is Summon® Suggestions, a set of contextual research assistance services. These features use data from

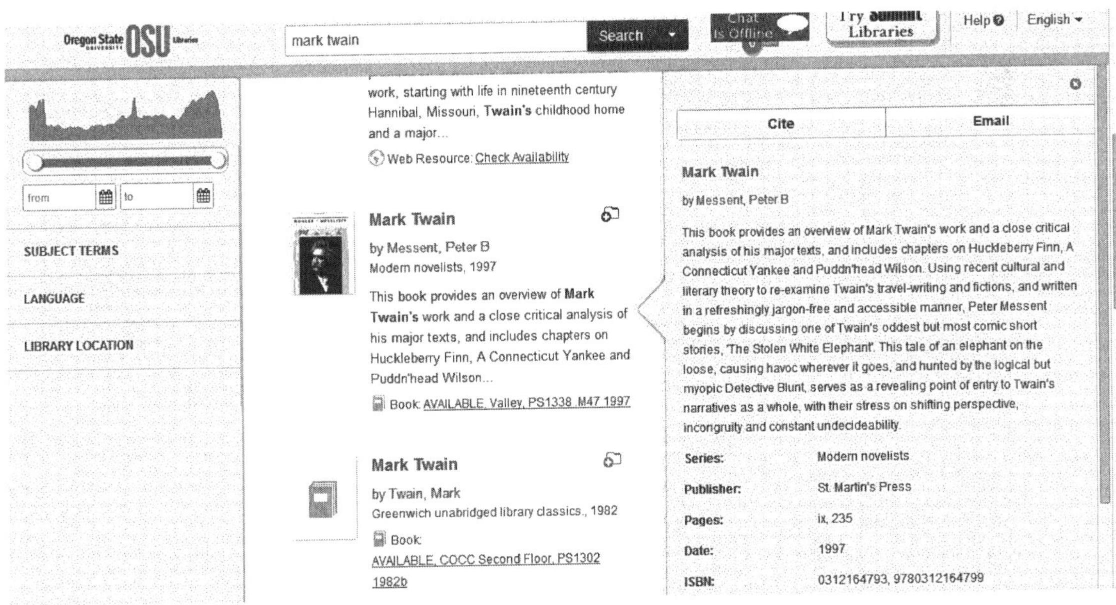

Figure 2.5. Full record view from Oregon State University Libraries' Summon Service. *Courtesy Oregon State University Libraries, Oregon State University, Corvallis, OR.*

searches and full-text views on Summon systems, input from the local library staff, and the Summon community at large. A Database Recommender analyzes the search and retrieval and recommends subject databases that the searcher could consider searching directly for more or better results. Related Searches suggests related concepts or search terms, and Autocomplete shows frequently searched concepts based on the first word input. Because the suggestions come from the Summon community, they are generally academic focused and frequently multilingual. Best Bets recommendations are controlled by the local library and can be used to promote particular resources or collections.

Summon 2.0, released in 2013, introduced several new enhanced content features, including Summon Topic Explorer™ and Summon Scholar Profiles™. The Topic Explorer can be customized by the library, and it opens a separate pane of content related to the search topic, which can include encyclopedia and other reference source material (see figure 2.6), LibGuides, and subject librarian profiles. Scholar Profiles brings content from ProQuest's Scholar Universe to supply additional information about key authors and researchers.

API, Customization, and Mobile Features

Like many other WSD products, ProQuest provides opportunities to tailor and customize the interface. Customers can easily add a hyperlinked library logo to all Summon pages, and a Summon Customizer feature allows custom HTML, including style sheets to be added to the header and footer of pages (Vaughan 2011b). For those who desire a highly customized interface, ProQuest offers the Summon application programming interface (API), which exposes virtually all of Summon's functionality and provides opportunity to make local changes. Oregon State University Library programming staff detailed their experience customizing Summon with API in an article for Code4Lib in 2010. They tailored the content of MARC item records displayed and customized their list of location codes (Klein 2010). Summon also includes

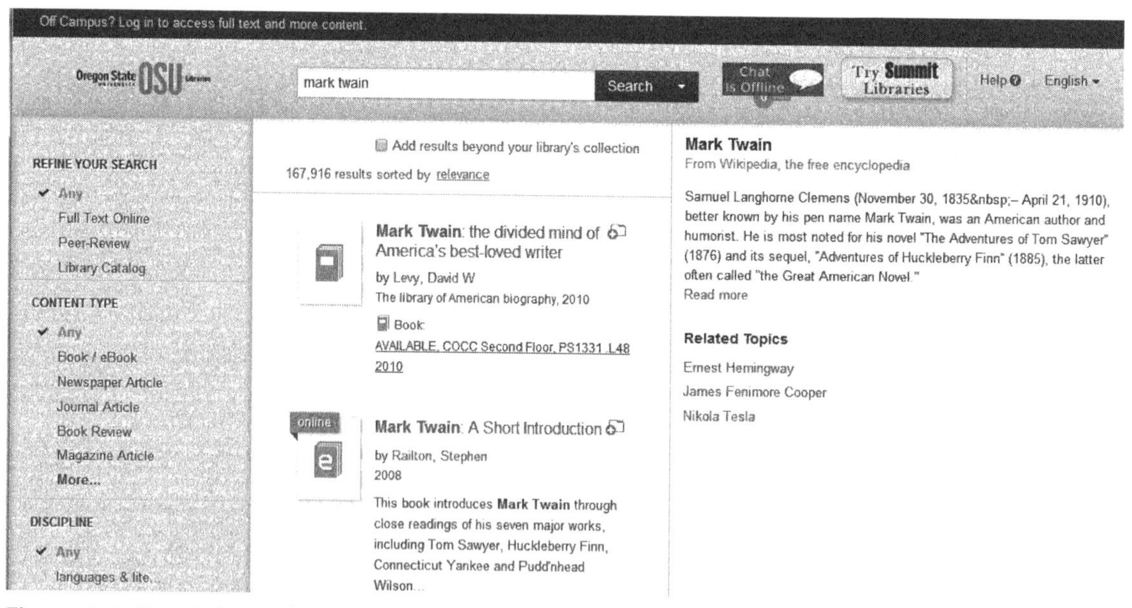

Figure 2.6. Search for Mark Twain on Oregon State University Libraries' Summon Service. *Courtesy Oregon State University Libraries, Oregon State University, Corvallis, OR.*

a responsive mobile interface that recognizes and adjusts for display on mobile devices with no apps required.

Platform and Purchasing Options

Summon is available exclusively as a hosted (cloud based) service. Updates are delivered approximately quarterly. Pricing is by annual subscription, and discounts are available for multiyear contracts and consortia participants. The pricing formula gives consideration to the number of FTEs and degree-granting status of the institution. Summon was reported to be in 704 libraries worldwide in 2013 (Breeding 2014). The majority of customers are academic libraries. More information about Summon is available at http://www.serials-solutions.com/en/services/summon.

Recent publications about Summon include the following:

Buck, Stefanie, and Margaret Mellinger. 2011. "The Impact of Serial Solutions' Summon™ on Information Literacy Instruction: Librarian Perceptions." *Internet Reference Services Quarterly* 16, no. 4: 159–81.

Cardwell, Catherine, Vera Lux, and Robert J Snyder. 2012. "Beyond Simple, Easy, and Fast: Reflections on Teaching Summon." *College & Research Libraries News* 73, no. 6: 344–47.

Newcomer, Nara L. 2011. "Summon." *Music Reference Services Quarterly* 14, nos. 1–2: 59–62.

Stone, Graham. 2010. "Searching Life, the Universe and Everything? The Implementation of Summon at the University of Huddersfield." *Liber Quarterly: The Journal of European Research Libraries* 20, no. 1: 25–51.

Vaughan, Jason. 2011. "Serials Solutions Summon." *Library Technology Reports* 47, no. 1: 22–29.

WorldCat Discovery Service, OCLC

Product Overview and Brief History

Though Summon often gets credit for being the first WSD system, WorldCat Discovery Service (formerly WorldCat Local) predated it by nearly two years. In his Library Technology Reports issue on WSD systems, Jason Vaughan (2011c) wrote that WorldCat Local had all the hallmarks of a WSD system when it launched the service in early 2007 as a pilot program for the University of Washington library system. OCLC combined the WorldCat database and its article-level records from FirstSearch into a customized system that put the university's locally held records at the top of relevancy rankings and incorporated the institution's branding. OCLC began marketing the product the same year.

WorldCat Local originally came in two versions. WorldCat Local "quickstart" was offered to all FirstSearch subscribers for free. It was scaled down in its services for consortia subscribers in particular but offered customized branding and a search box that libraries could place on any webpage. Both it and the full WorldCat Local looked and functioned very similarly to WorldCat generally, with many of the same discovery layer features. In January 2014, OCLC announced that it would launch WorldCat Discovery Services in March. The new service replaces WorldCat Local, quickstart, and FirstSearch. All FirstSearch and WorldCat Local subscribers will be transferred to WorldCat Discovery Service over the course of 2014 (OCLC 2014).

WorldCat Discovery Service was created with the input of customers of both FirstSearch and WorldCat Local, with 650 libraries participating as beta testers. Some of the

TEXTBOX 2.1.

FURTHER INFORMATION FROM OCLC ON THE TRANSITION FROM FIRSTSEARCH AND WORLDCAT LOCAL TO WORLDCAT DISCOVERY SERVICE

In March 2014, OCLC will release WorldCat® Discovery Services, a new suite of cloud-based applications that brings the FirstSearch® and WorldCat® Local services together. The new suite will enable people to discover more than 1.5 billion electronic, digital, and physical resources in libraries around the world through a single search of both WorldCat® and a central index that represents nearly 2,000 e-content collections. This will make it possible for the more than 18,000 FirstSearch libraries to offer a richer discovery experience to their users.

WorldCat Discovery Services will bring together access for all electronic, digital, and physical collections in a single interface, optimized for use across desktops, laptops, tablets, and smartphones. It will be available to all current FirstSearch subscribers in March 2014 as part of existing subscriptions.

FirstSearch will operate in parallel with WorldCat Discovery during a yearlong transition, allowing libraries to choose their transition timing. Current WorldCat Local and WorldShare® Management Services libraries can begin to use WorldCat Discovery Services during a beta period that begins in April 2014. WorldCat Discovery Services can also be tailored to enhance the local discovery experience through additional fee-based options.

biggest changes include a free integrated A-Z list for FirstSearch users and fee-based options to customize and tailor the interface for the local environment.

Central Index Content

In 2009, perhaps in reaction to the introduction of Summon, OCLC vastly expanded its content base by forming publisher partnership agreements with EBSCO, RR Bowker, and HW Wilson, among others. Its website states that WorldCat Discovery Service now includes 2 billion electronic, digital, and physical resource records in libraries around the world. Major content sources include ArticleFirst, JSTOR, Elsevier, OAister, MEDLINE, ebrary, LexisNexis, and HathiTrust along with all the content available in WorldCat itself. Further details on content sources are available at http://www.oclc.org/worldcatlocal/overview/content/default.htm. EBSCO, Gale, and ProQuest content is also available for mutually subscribing libraries.

Integration of Local and Catalog Content

Because most libraries already have their full holdings in OCLC, there is usually no need for subscribing libraries to load local catalog records on a regular basis. OCLC offers a free onetime reclamation process for libraries to update holdings if they have not been kept current. Other local collections, such as digital repositories, will need to be loaded regularly. OCLC supports OAI-PMH and CONTENTdm compliant sources, converting them to MARC for inclusion in the central index. The knowledge base allows pulling of live location and status information from the library's ILS into local catalog record display in WorldCat Discovery Service. This service will be provided for a fee for former FirstSearch subscribers. Other new fee-based services include course reserves management and reading lists.

Unlike other WSD systems, WorldCat Discovery Service exploits the WorldCat database to show users other geographically local libraries that hold an item when it is not currently available from the home library. OCLC also allows the library to designate a second tier of related libraries whose collections display after the library's collection holdings and before WorldCat's geographically local collections generally. This can be handy for consortial groups or libraries that have collection development or document delivery arrangements with other libraries. When launching the search, users can designate which collections to include in the search.

Relevancy Ranking and Metadata

WorldCat Discovery Service defaults to keyword searches on MARC tags but not full text. Proximity of search terms and inclusion in key fields, such as the title, author, or subject, boost relevancy ranking, as do item currency and inclusion in the library's collections.

Retrieval Display, Refinement, and Management Features

WorldCat Discovery Service includes facet sets, relevancy ranking, and results sorting. Results are presented in a two-column view with facets to the left (see figure 2.7). Users can change the sort (to library, author, title or date), save results to a list, or save the search query.

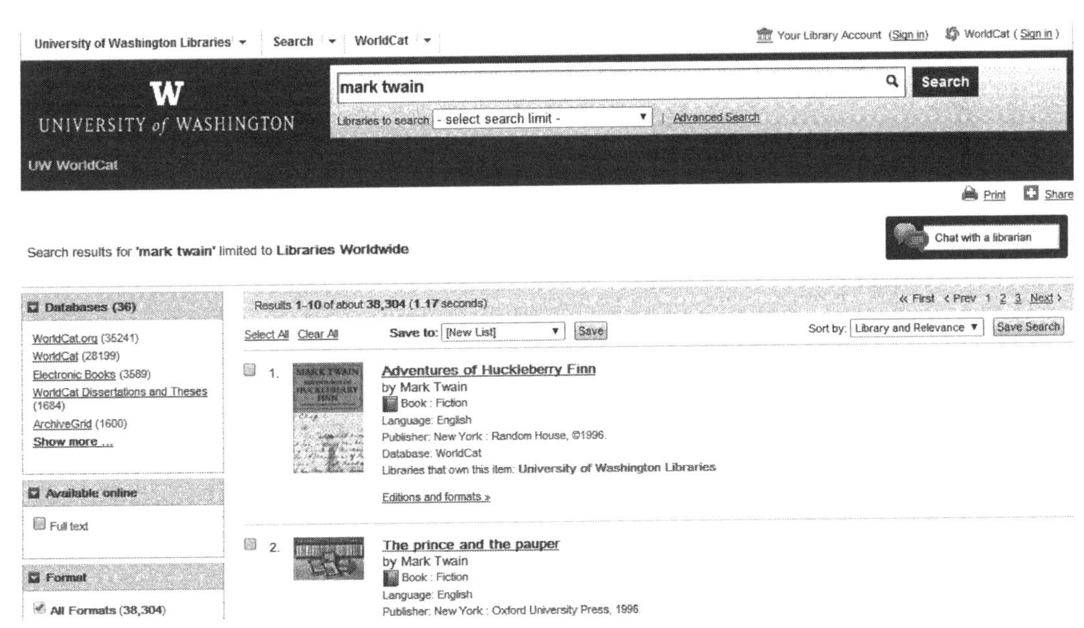

Figure 2.7. Search for Mark Twain on the University of Washington's WorldCat Local Service. © *2014 OCLC Online Computer Library Center, Inc., used with the permission of OCLC and University of Washington Libraries, University of Washington, Seattle, WA; WorldCat, WorldCat.org, and the WorldCat logo are registered trademarks/service marks of OCLC.*

Libraries can set up a local knowledge base that integrates full-text delivery options either through the library's URL resolver or requests to the library's document delivery services. WorldCat Discovery Service will make automated linking available for libraries that maintain local holdings in WorldCat. For print records, local item holdings are displayed first, followed by holdings of the second-tier libraries and, finally, from WorldCat libraries generally.

WorldCat Discovery Service has a full suite of postsearch saving and processing features. Users can save a citation in a variety of formats, export (to RefWorks, EndNote or EasyBib), e-mail, share to a number of social networking sites (including Facebook, Twitter, and LinkedIn), or save a permalink (see figure 2.8). Users can set up an account to use the Shopping Cart features, including saving to "Things I Own" or "Things to Check Out" lists. Users can add notes and tags to lists or opt to make them viewable by anyone or kept private.

Social Media, Recommender, and Special Content Features

WorldCat Discovery Service includes book jacket art and other enhanced content, such as summaries and TOCs from Google Books. Libraries can alternatively choose to subscribe to a Syndetics-enhanced content package either through OCLC or through Syndetics directly. Reviews from third-party editorial and social media services such as WeRead and GoodReads are available if the subscribing library chooses to enable them. WorldCat Discovery Service also has integrated user tagging and review services native to the interface, and users can create a personal profile that includes a picture and interests.

WorldCat Discovery pulls additional content into the full record display to enhance bibliographic records. Clicking on the author tag brings up a page that includes the

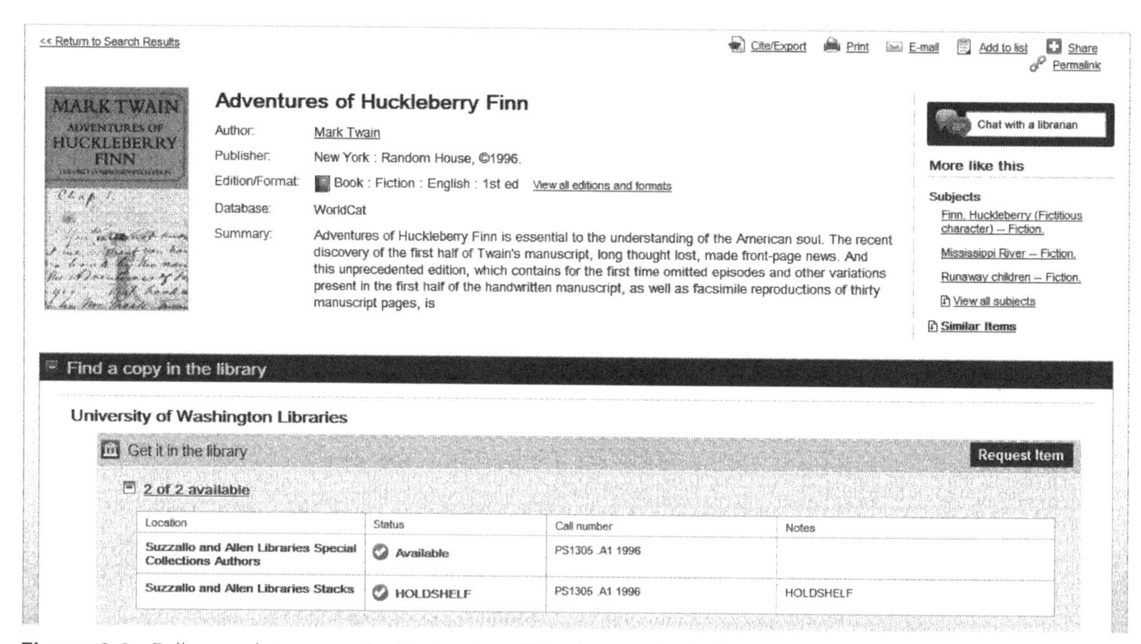

Figure 2.8. Full record view on the University of Washington's WorldCat Local Service. *© 2014 OCLC Online Computer Library Center, Inc., used with the permission of OCLC and University of Washington Libraries, University of Washington, Seattle, WA; WorldCat, WorldCat.org, and the WorldCat logo are registered trademarks/service marks of OCLC.*

author's publication timeline and most widely held works. FRBR features display and provide links to additional forms and editions of the work.

In 2008, OCLC and Google entered into an agreement to essentially share data. WorldCat records are displayed in Google Books searches, and Google Books content is integrated into WorldCat services. This means that a local searcher can see a library's holdings represented in Google Books and general Google results lists. Millions of scanned books from the Google Books project are available in the WorldCat Discovery Service central index. OCLC has also formed partnerships with Yahoo Search and Bing Search to index WorldCat content, making local library collections available through searches of these popular services. More recently, OCLC began including schema.org linked data for all WorldCat records, which exposes WorldCat records more effectively in search engine results generally.

API, Customization, and Mobile Features

OCLC has several well-documented APIs that can be used for WorldCat Discovery Service. These include WorldCat Search API, WorldCat Metadata API, WorldCat Recommender Service API, and WorldCat knowledge base API. More information on these can be found at http://www.oclc.org/developer/develop/web-services.en.html.

WorldCat Discovery Service has a mobile interface that does not require app purchase or installation. Mobile-optimized views are supported for a variety of devices, including most smartphones and browser applications for tablet devices. Libraries can create a custom mobile website, and subscribers can develop up to 10 URLs for custom mobile sites.

Platform and Purchasing Options

WorldCat Discovery Service is offered exclusively as a cloud-based service. OCLC recently expanded its cloud services for libraries beyond discovery with its WorldShare Management Service (WMS), offering acquisitions, license management, and circulation services in place of a traditional integrated library system. Collaboration and record sharing are at the heart of OCLC services, and web scale enables the large-scale data-hosting platform for this cooperative environment.

Libraries should contact their OCLC service representatives to get a quote for implementation and subscription services pricing. OCLC reported WorldCat Local in 1,717 libraries as of March 2014. With the transition to WorldCat Discovery Service, bringing many FirstSearch libraries to the new platform, this number should increase significantly over the course of the year. More information about WorldCat Discovery Service is available at http://www.oclc.org/worldcat_discovery.en.html.

Recent publications about WorldCat Local/WorldCat Discovery Service include the following:

Bertot, John Carlo, Katie Berube, Peter Devereaux, et al. 2012. "Assessing the Usability of WorldCat Local: Findings and Considerations." *Library Quarterly* 82, no. 2 (April): 207–21.

Fahey, Sue, Shannon Gordon, and Crystal Rose. 2011. "Seeing Double at Memorial University: Two WorldCat Local Usability Studies." *Partnership: The Canadian Journal of Library and Information Practice and Research* 6, no. 2: 1–14.

Grotti, Margaret G., and Karen Sobel. 2012. "WorldCat Local and Information Literacy Instruction: An Exploration of Emerging Teaching Practice." *Public Services Quarterly* 8, no. 1: 12–25.

OCLC. 2014. *OCLC Introduces WorldCat Discovery Services* (news release). January 22. http://www.oclc.org/news/releases/2014/201403dublin.en.html.
Thomas, Bob, and Stefanie Buck. 2010. "OCLC's WorldCat Local versus III's WebPAC." *Library Hi Tech* 28, no. 4: 648–71.
Vaughan, Jason. 2011. "OCLC WorldCat Local." *Library Technology Reports* 47, no. 1: 12–21.

Examining Discovery Layer–Web-Scale Content Hybrids

In 2013 several integrated library system (ILS) vendors announced partnerships with EBSCO to deliver the central index content of EDS via the vendor's discovery layer/OPAC. These deals included Innovative Interfaces, which married its popular Encore next-generation catalog/discovery system with EDS content, and SirsiDynix, which did the same with its Enterprise discovery layer (Sabrosky 2012). Since then, EBSCO formed similar relationships with many other ILS vendors to deliver EDS content to its catalog interfaces. Currently, it lists more than 20 vendors that are participating on its website, including EOS, Kuali Ole, Softlink, Talis, and OCLC.

This new type of partnership, being referred to here as a "hybrid system," combines the features of an established discovery layer with the central index content offered up by a service like EDS. Prospective buyers should understand that they are not purchasing the full discovery features of EDS. An EBSCO Publishing press release about the joint venture with Innovative indicates that the product will integrate EDS content and relevancy ranking and "the features and functionality that have come to define EBSCO Discovery Service" (EBSCO 2012). Which features will be included and which will not are hard to determine, as this product is just out of beta.

The emergence of hybrid systems are reflective of the fact that many libraries implemented next-gen catalog services such as Encore and Enterprise and spent a good deal of time customizing these interfaces for optimal use by their patrons. In a fast-moving environment, their patrons have just gotten used to the new discovery interface, and libraries may prefer to keep what they have in place and simply enhance it with improved access to a robust electronic content collection.

Another advantage of these hybrids is a tighter integration of catalog data and services. EDS does not offer the ability to place holds on library materials or allow users to see what they have checked out or renew materials. To perform these functions, the user must link to the catalog record in the library's native OPAC service. Encore and Enterprise both provide these services, since they are in effect an enhanced OPAC product. ProQuest's Summon is working to develop an interface that would allow these services to be offered directly within Summon, rather than forcing the user to link out to the OPAC. Libraries using Encore and Enterprise as the discovery layer to Innovative and SirsiDynix ILS products, respectively, also would not have to do regular loads of catalog data or set up Z39.50 calls or screen scraping of the OPAC to provide live status information for catalog records.

Because EDS, Summon, and Primo have robust APIs in place, libraries with the programming resources can already pull content from these services into other discovery layers or OPACs. This has been done by a number of VuFind libraries. VuFind is an open-source next-gen catalog/discovery layer that was developed by Villanova University in 2007. Libraries that purchase open-source products frequently have the programming

TEXTBOX 2.2.

INDEPENDENT DISCOVERY LAYERS

These discovery layers are sold or available open source independent from an integrated library system or complete WSD product. Some can be populated with EDS, WorldCat, Primo Central, or Summon central index content through API. Others can be configured to include catalog, local collections, and article-level content via federated search. This is not a comprehensive list but includes those commonly found in U.S. libraries.

Aquabrowser: One of the most widely adopted next-generation OPAC products, it is still available for purchase from Serials Solutions/ProQuest but being displaced by improvements to native ILS OPAC interfaces and more comprehensive discovery competitors. http://www.serialssolutions.com/en/services/aquabrowser

Bibliocore: An independent discovery layer developed with the needs of public libraries in mind, putting an emphasis on social media integration. Commonly adopted by public library systems, including New York Public Library. http://www.bibliocommons.com

Blacklight: An open-source discovery layer developed by the University of Virginia. It is known for its tailored presentation of different formats, making it appealing for libraries with special collections. Used mostly by academic and special libraries. http://projectblacklight.org

Encore: Marketed initially as a next-generation catalog layer from Innovative Interfaces, it can be purchased separately from Innovative's ILS products. It will ingest local content from a variety of sources and is now capable of integrating EDS content. Encore Synergy is also available, which uses web services technology to deliver article-level content from databases and aggregators. Encore is used in academic, public, and special libraries. http://iii.com/products/encore

VuFind: VuFind was developed by Villanova University as a next-generation OPAC and is frequently implemented as an independent front end to Summon, WorldCat, and other content sources. It is used by both academic and public libraries. http://www.vufind.org

workforce and entrepreneurial spirit to exploit the opportunities presented by open-source code and APIs. In a 2012 *Ariadne* article, Graham Seaman (2012), of Royal Halloway Library, University of London, described its project to combine VuFind and Summon. Villanova University Library and the Bridge Consortium (Carleton and St. Olaf colleges) both did the same, opting to keep VuFind in place but enhance it with Summon content. The VuFind website offers developers code for combining VuFind with Summon and WorldCat. EDS, Primo, and Summon API's also make integration with other independent and open-source discovery layers possible.

Exploring Web-Scale Discovery Alternatives

Some traditional ILS vendors have developed alternative technologies that bring article-level integration into their OPAC/next-gen catalog products. SirsiDynix relies on federated search via ProQuest's 360 Search Service to bring article-level content to its next-gen catalog product, Enterprise. Enterprise will also do web crawling to discover and pull links to websites and PDFs into search results. SirsiDynix developed a "fuzzy logic" formula to relevance rank results and features facets, "Did you mean?" suggestions, and auto-complete to help searchers find results. Customers can add third-party content for social media services such as tagging and user reviews, and it integrates with Syndetics ICE enhanced content to deliver jacket art, table of contents, excerpts, and author notes. Auto-Graphics AGent Search and TLC's LS2 PAC also provide options to bring article-level results into these OPAC products via federated search (Luther and Kelly 2011).

Innovative Interfaces applied a different technology to bring article-level results into its Encore Synergy product, released in the spring of 2010. It uses real-time web services connections to content providers to retrieve article content. Instead of directly interfiling article and catalog results, Encore shows just a preview set of articles in the middle of the catalog search results, which are listed by relevancy ranking (Breeding 2010). Innovative considers this an advantage over the competition, asserting that its system does not drown out the book and multimedia sources that often get lost in the volume of heavier metadata from full-text article content. If searchers want to pursue more article content based on the preview, they can click through to the full-articles result set. Innovative entered into partnerships with a number of publisher content providers, including Gale, LexisNexis, Elsevier, ProQuest, and JSTOR, to deliver its article content via the Synergy web services connectors. Encore Synergy can be configured to import records from any

TEXTBOX 2.3.

RECOMMENDED FURTHER READING: RESULTS OF BREEDING'S 2013 LIBRARY DISCOVERY SURVEY

In 2013, Marshall Breeding included a survey of library discovery services on his Library Technology Guides website. Library subscribers or purchasers of the products responded to questions assessing:

- General satisfaction
- Effectiveness by user population (undergraduate, faculty, general public)
- Comprehensiveness of scope
- Effectiveness of relevancy ranking
- Objective search performance

Results were reported in Library Technology Reports (50, no. 1, "Major Discovery Product Profiles," pp. 33–52). Breeding (2013) also includes comments from respondents about each product. All the web-scale discovery services were included, along with other popular discovery layers (Encore, Enterprise, Bibliocommons, etc.).

integrated library system, but the tightest integration will be with libraries that are Millennium or Sierra customers.

At this time, libraries have a number of choices if they want to offer their patrons a one-stop search tool. Hybrids and alternative products may offer the best match for the needs of libraries that do not find a good fit with one of the four WSD services currently available.

Key Points

Four full-fledged web-scale discovery products are currently on the market: EBSCO Discovery Service (EDS), Primo (with Primo Central content), Summon, and WorldCat Discovery Service (formerly WorldCat Local). All offer robust central index content, integration of local content, and extensive discovery layer features. Most include social media content, tagging, and recommender services. All can be customized and branded and include an API layer and mobile interfaces.

Hybrid systems that marry the content of a web-scale discovery service with a different discovery layer are just starting to come to the market. Libraries that are Innovative Interfaces or SirsiDynix customers may also want to consider Encore Synergy or Enterprise as alternatives. These products use federated search and web services technologies to bring article-level content to each vendor's next-gen catalog services.

References

Breeding, Marshall. 2009. "Summon: A New Search Service from Serials Solutions." Smart Libraries Newsletter 29, no. 3: 1–3. http://www.librarytechnology.org/ltg-displaytext.pl?RC=14000.

———. 2010. "Access Articles through Encore Synergy." *Smart Libraries Newsletter* 30, no. 6: 2–4. http://www.librarytechnology.org/ltg-displaytext.pl?RC=16251.

———. 2013. "Discovery Layer Interfaces." *Library Technology Guides*. http://www.librarytechnology.org/discovery.pl.

———. 2014. "Major Discovery Product Profiles." *Library Technology Reports* 50, no. 1: 32–55.

Brynko, Barbara. 2011. "EDS: A Single Point of Discovery." *Information Today* 28, no. 3: 33. http://www.infotoday.com/it/mar11/EDS-A-Single-Point-of-Discovery.shtml.

Dartmouth College Library. 2009. "An Evaluation of Serials Solutions Summon as a Discovery Service for the Dartmouth College Library." November 10. http://www.dartmouth.edu/~library/admin/docs/Summon_Report.pdf.

EBSCO. 2012. "EBSCO Publishing and Innovative Interfaces Expand Partnership with EBSCO Discovery Service and Encore." Press release. June 22. http://www.ebscohost.com/newsroom/stories/ebsco-publishing-and-innovative-interfaces-expand-partnership.

Hadro, Josh. 2009. "Serials Solutions Announces Summon, A New Unified Discovery Interface." *Library Journal*. January 20. http://www.libraryjournal.com/article/CA6630537.html.

Klein, Michael B. 2010. "Hacking Summon." *code4lib Journal* 11 (September 21). http://journal.code4lib.org/articles/3655.

Luther, Judy, and Maureen C. Kelly. 2011. "The Next Generation of Discovery." *Library Journal* 136, no. 5. http://www.libraryjournal.com/lj/home/889250-264/the_next_generation_of_discovery.html.csp.

OCLC. 2014. "OCLC Introduces WorldCat Discovery Services." News release. January 22. http://www.oclc.org/news/releases/2014/201403dublin.en.html.

Peterson-Sloss, Celeste. 2012. "Summon Adds New Capabilities." *Computers in Libraries* 32, no. 7, 38.
Rapp, David. 2010. "InfoTech." *Library Journal* 135, no. 17: 14.
Sabrosky, Suzanne. 2012. "Industry News: EBSCO*host*." *Online* 36, no. 5 (September): 8.
Schneider, K. G. 2009. "A Dozen Neat Take-Aways from ALA Midwinter 2009." *Free Range Librarian Blog*. February 2. http://freerangelibrarian.com/2009/02/02/a-dozen-from-ala-midwinter-2009/.
Seaman, Graham. 2012. "Adapting VuFind as a Front-End to a Commercial Discovery System." *Ariadne* 68 (March). http://www.ariadne.ac.uk/issue68/seaman.
Vaughan, Jason. 2011a. "Ex Libris Primo Central." *Library Technology Reports* 47, no. 1: 39–47.
———. 2011b. "OCLC WorldCat Local." *Library Technology Reports* 47 no. 1: 12–21.
———. 2011c. "Serials Solutions Summon." *Library Technology Reports* 47, no. 1: 22–29.

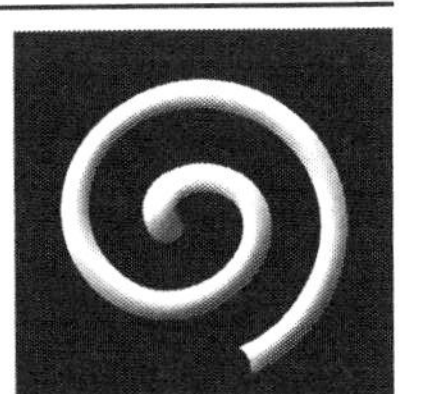

CHAPTER 3

Making the Best Content Match for Your Library

IN THIS CHAPTER

- ▷ Defining the Audience for Web-Scale Discovery
- ▷ Doing an Effective Content Analysis
- ▷ Integrating Catalog and Other Local Data

ONCE A LIBRARY DETERMINES THAT WEB-SCALE DISCOVERY is a service that it would like to provide for its user population, the next step is to determine which available products will be the best fit for the local environment. The content included is one of the most important considerations. Though the four web-scale discovery services on the market have much content in common, each has its own strengths and focuses. Summon is particularly strong on news sources, based on the ProQuest content at its core. Similarly, WorldCat Discovery Service is strong on covering the holdings of libraries all over the world. Making the best content match for library users and the local environment is a complex process. This chapter provides evaluation points to consider when making this assessment.

Defining the Audience for Web-Scale Discovery

The population target for web-scale discovery can vary greatly from library to library. At academic institutions, the early perceived audience was undergraduate students. These students have research and classwork needs that can typically be met by a web-scale discovery (WSD) service. At the same time, they are the population at greatest need for an easy-to-navigate system that leads them to reputable resources. Head and Eisenberg reported in 2009 that these students frequently are "confused and frustrated by the research process . . . having particular difficulty traversing a vast and ever-changing information landscape." They will often turn to Google or Google Scholar as their first and primary research tool.

Though undergraduates are typically the target in an academic environment, WSD services have the potential to meet the specified needs of graduate students and faculty. A WSD service can be a great starting point when the searcher is working on interdisciplinary research or a topic that is not her or his primary area of focus (Luther and Kelly 2011). WSD services, particularly those with database recommender features, can also help guide searchers to the best databases for a deeper search. Jeff Daniels, of Grand Valley State University, praised Summon's database recommender for directing patrons to the best subject-specific resources (Daniels, Robinson, and Wishnetsky 2013).

In special, corporate, or academic libraries with particular subject foci (e.g., law, health sciences), a WSD service can meet these wide net–casting search needs. Searchers in these environments will often turn to Google as a starting point or if they require a quick answer to a question. A WSD service could be a better choice if it can be tailored by customization to meet the needs of a subject-specific environment.

WSD service purchasers should determine the following about the audience for the search tool to make sure that content needs can be met by a prospective product.

- What are the most used and important databases and electronic resource packages that the library subscribes to or purchases? Are the users of these content sources included in the target audience for the WSD service?
- Similarly, what publishers, journals, and e-book packages are critical for the target audience?
- In public libraries, university, and other nonspecialized academic libraries, should the WSD service include just the most commonly used sources for quick answers targeted at a general audience, or should it be as complete as possible (covering as much of the library's purchased and subscription content)?
- If in a special library or specialized academic environment, should the WSD service be customizable to eliminate content that may not be of value to searchers while including as much of the desired content as possible?
- If the library serves a wide range of users with differing needs, should the WSD service be configured with multiple profiles, offering unique sets of content to serve specific groups?

Doing an Effective Content Analysis

Key Content Analysis Considerations

- What should be requested in a vendor content analysis?
- How much of the content is exclusive to the service?
- What e-book content is included?
- Can specialized content can be integrated?
- How much of the original source or A&I metadata is available for searching?
- Can undesired content be suppressed?
- Are multiple specialized profiles an option?

Determining exactly what content is included in a particular web-scale discovery service is one of the most difficult parts of assessing one of these systems. Content comparison is generally not an "apples to apples" affair. While librarians tend to think in terms of contents of a particular database or matching on a title list, that is often not an easy way to assess WSD content:

> While it's possible to determine which databases or individual titles are included, a detailed comparison of discovery services at the title level is an overwhelming task, as coverage of titles varies based on the depth of the archive and the currency of the content. (Luther and Kelly 2011)

When inquiring about inclusion of a particular database, the vendor may say that a certain percentage of the database is included in the central index content but some key metadata may not be searchable (Hoeppner 2012). Likewise, going by total number of titles or items indexed is not going to provide an accurate assessment of whether the key content required is actually included. A recent movement toward standards for contribution and disclosure of content in these systems may improve transparency in the future (see "Emerging Standards for Web-Scale Discovery" in chapter 12). Asking the following questions of multiple vendors will help determine a good match to needed resources.

What Should Be Requested in a Vendor Content Analysis?

Most vendors are able to provide an analysis of coverage based on lists of key databases and publishers through which the library purchases large volumes of subscriptions or electronic resource package subscriptions. The analysis is free and can be requested during the evaluation phase of the project. Vaughan (2011b) recommends asking the following during a content analysis:

- Has the vendor established a partnership arrangement with the publisher to harvest content and metadata? Are these agreements indefinite, or do they have expiration dates?
- Is the content included in the central index or some other method?
- What level of metadata is provided and discoverable?
- How many titles are included for each publisher?

It is possible to request an analysis based on a title list. Request what years of publication are included, what metadata is harvested, and if the full-text content is searchable for all desired publication years. ProQuest makes a title list available on its website for evaluation by prospective subscribers of Summon. However, this document is thousands of pages long and growing, making a title-by-title comparison a labor-intensive activity, especially for libraries with large serial collections and extensive electronic subscriptions.

How Much of the Content Is Exclusive to the Service?

As competition heats up among the vendors, being able to claim exclusive rights to a particular publisher's catalog or highly sought resource is a selling point. EDS and Summon in

TEXTBOX 3.1.

CENTRAL INDEX CONTENT SOURCES

- Contributed publisher content
- Contributed aggregator content
- Open-source content (Hathi Trust, WorldCat, etc.)
- Local content (catalog records, digital collections, institutional repositories, etc.)

Content is "preharvested" and normalized to common metadata fields for indexing. This results in faster search results.

particular are likely to hold exclusive rights to EBSCO*host* databases (EDS) or ProQuest content (Summon):

> Neither one contributes their A&I products to the other's discovery service, leading to the problem of both having to cover that material in other ways in their discovery service. Ex Libris is impacted even more, since neither EBSCO nor ProQuest contribute to Ex Libris's Primo Central index. (Kelley 2012)

This issue of exclusive content is currently being challenged on several fronts. Large and influential WSD service subscribers are requesting that aggregators and A&I (abstract and indexing) databases make their content available to all discovery services (Grant 2013). Proposed standards for discovery services are also taking on the content status quo (Kelley 2012). More discussion of this issue is included in "Moving Toward a More Equitable Content Environment" (chapter 12). For now, it is best to ask vendors what exclusive content is held and what subject areas or material types are particularly well represented.

What E-book Content Is Included?

As libraries expand their e-book collections, having full-text access to this content is increasingly important. Many WSD services include Google Books, WorldCat, and Hathi Trust among their open-access content sources. But coverage of paid e-book packages may be affected by who controls the content. ProQuest completed full-text indexing of ebrary in 2012, making its titles available for search in Summon (ProQuest 2013). Because this is ProQuest owned content, it likely will not be available to all WSD providers. Check with the vendor specifically about full-text coverage of the library's critical e-book packages. Also inquire about integration of e-book lending interfaces.

Can Specialized Content Can Be Integrated?

Special libraries and large academics frequently have extremely specialized content that may not be included in the WSD service's central index. Inquire if there are ways to incorporate these sources through a link out to the database, federated search, or creating connectors to integrate the results. The Integrated Search feature in EDS will display the number of hits in selected external databases and allow users to integrate the retrieval in the results list (Hoeppner 2012). Creating custom connectors like this is usually an added expense, unless another library has already had the programming done.

How Much of the Original Source or A&I Metadata Is Available for Searching?

As Hoeppner illustrated in her 2012 article on evaluating WSD services, the metadata available in an A&I database record is sometimes stripped down or restructured when it is "normalized" for a WSD central index. The American Psychological Association does not supply PsycINFO to most WSD services; however, it does supply the full-text PsycARTICLES, PsycBOOKS, and PsycCritiques to all four. Other A&I database services are not providing records to WSD services out of fear that their records are not adequately discoverable in this search environment and that low reported usage might lead to cancellation of the native search interface.

> "The producers of these products work hard to ensure that they work well when used through their own interfaces," Breeding says. "When the data that underlie the A&I products are incorporated into a broader discovery service, it may or may not appear with the kind of weighting that would apply within the original interface, and it may not be clear to the researcher that the citation came from their product." (Kelley 2012, 6)

The Bibliography of Asian Studies, an A&I database directed at a specialized audience, is not included in the four WSD services. However, many of the citations in that database are covered in other A&I databases, and publishers of journals indexed may have contributed full text to one or several of the WSD services. Figure 3.1 is an illustration of how one record in the A&I database is included in Summon and EDS. Summon has the record from Social Science Citation Index. EDS has the record from two sources: JSTOR Arts and Sciences I and Academic Search Premier. The metadata included in each of these records is different.

Ask the vendor how indexing from key A&I databases is handled and if searching of abstract contents or the full-text source documents is available. Sometimes the frequency of word occurrence in documents that is used by many relevancy-ranking algorithms can boost less relevant documents and obscure subject indexing for more relevant documents. This should be considered in environments where A&I database content that does not include abstracts and full text is important and if quality subject indexing is highly valued.

Can Undesired Content Be Suppressed?

Most services will likely have some content that is not of top priority to a library's users, especially in a special library situation. One category of content that can dominate search results is news. Summon, which has a lot of news content, has a built-in filter that can be enabled to block news content if desired. EDS, which draws heavily from EBSCO*host* databases, allows libraries to selectively choose the EBSCO*host* databases that feed into search results.

Another consideration is how much of the central index content is mutually licensed. If a WSD service includes content that the library does not subscribe to, users will be

A&I Database: Bibliography of Asian Studies

Refugees, land reclamation, and militarized landscapes in wartime China: Huanglongshan, Shaanxi, 1937-45
By: Muscolino, Micah S.
Journal: *Journal of Asian Studies* 69, no.2 (May 2010) p. 453-478
Keywords: refugee flight; wartime environmental change; Sino-Japanese War (1937-1945); land clearance; resettlement of Yellow River flood refugees; wartime mobilization; deforestation; susceptibility to disease; Keshan disease; population displacement
Subjects: China -- History -- By Period -- Republic (1911-1949)
China -- Science & Technology -- Environmental Studies
China -- Economics -- Land Development & Settlement
China -- Anthropology & Sociology -- Social Change
China -- Science & Technology -- Medicine

Summon/Proquest: Source of the Record – Social Science Citation Index

Title: Refugees, Land Reclamation, and Militarized Landscapes in Wartime China: Huanglongshan, Shaanxi, 1937-45
Author: Muscolino, Micah S
Publication title: The Journal of Asian Studies
Volume: 69
Issue: 2
Pages 453-478
Number of pages 26
Publication year 2010
Publication date: May 2010
Year: 2010
Subjects: Refugees; Land reclamation; Armed forces;War
Location: China
Publication subject: Social Sciences: Comprehensive Works, Political Science--International Relations, Asian Studies, Literature

EDS: Source of the Record - JSTOR

Title: Refugees, Land Reclamation, and Militarized Landscapes in Wartime China: Huanglongshan, Shaanxi, 1937-45
Authors: MUSCOLINO, MICAH S.
Source: The Journal of Asian Studies. MAY 2010, Vol. 69, Issue 2, p453-478, 26p.
Subject Terms: Asian Studies

EDS: Source of the Record – Academic Search Premier

Title: Refugees, Land Reclamation, and Militarized Landscapes in Wartime China: Huanglongshan, Shaanxi, 1937-45.
Authors: MUSCOLINO, MICAH S.[1]
Source: Journal of Asian Studies. May2010, Vol. 69 Issue 2, p453-478. 26p.
Subject Terms:*SINO-Japanese War, 1937-1945; ***REFUGEES**; *RECLAMATION of land; *MILITARISM;
*POLITICAL leadership; *FORCED migration; *WAR & society; *HISTORY; QING dynasty, 1644-1912
Geographic Terms: SHAANXI Sheng (China), CHINA
Author Affiliations: Assistant Professor of History, Georgetown University.
ISSN: 00219118

Figure 3.1. Metadata from one article in an A&I database, Summon, and EDS.

able to search that content but will not be able to access the full text (Hoeppner 2012). If this includes a large percentage of the central index content, it may result in frustration by users who see results they want but then cannot get to the desired full text. Inquire if it is possible to block some of this content or default the system to automatically show just the results with full-text access. EDS can set this default with an option for the user to take it off if one wishes to see all results.

Are Multiple Specialized Profiles an Option?

For libraries that serve populations that have very different content needs, the ability to develop multiple profiles that address each may be highly desired. Inquire how content can be customized to meet the needs of particular groups. Can certain sources be turned on or off? Can connectors to critical sources outside the WSD service be tailored for a profile? Other considerations, such as unique facet groups or filter settings, may also be important. See the following chapter on discovery layer features for more information.

Integrating Catalog and Other Local Data

Beyond the central index content, local content sources such as catalog records are another vital source for most libraries that will implement web-scale discovery. What type of content the WSD service can ingest, how it makes these records searchable, and the process for loading these records should all be explored with the vendor. This will be particularly critical for libraries with specialized collections, such as music, archives, and art. Those with unique digital collections and institutional repositories will need to consider if these records should be included and how they will be handled.

What Is the Process for Loading Local Catalog Records?

Most WSD services require regular loading of bibliographic records from the local integrated library system to integrate them into the central index. Exceptions are for Primo subscribers who are on Ex Libris ILS products and for WorldCat Discovery Service subscribers who already include their catalog records in OCLC WorldCat. Otherwise, upload of records to a service can be done as frequently as daily if desired. Inquire how long it typically takes a new load to process. Large libraries that add volumes of records daily will be particularly affected.

As is the case with records coming from commercial services and publishers, there is often some normalization of the local bibliographic record. Inquire what parts of the records will remain discoverable, especially if the library adds unique local fields or, in the case of special libraries, has unusual formats and tags to accommodate. Also of importance is how index data is translated into facets and limits (e.g., what tags and subfields feed an author/creator facet). Inquire about the display of subfields in physical description tags where metadata embedded in these subfields could be of importance to users.

Libraries on the more common ILS products will find that the WSD vendors are well prepared for configuring record loading/calling and display of live location and status information for catalog records in the WSD service. Libraries on less common or homegrown systems should have a more serious dialogue with prospective vendors about record structure and where the fields for record match and holdings data can be located. Typically, match points are OCLC title control number (001 or 035 tags) or ISBN/ISSN. Holdings data is usually delivered in a 9xx tag, but libraries should check with their ILS vendor to confirm that this data can be easily output to one of these or an alternate tag.

What Other Local Data Can the Service Accommodate?

Many libraries have local content beyond the catalog that they may wish to include in a WSD service. This frequently consists of institutional repositories, digital collections, and other locally built and maintained databases. Most WSD services can accommodate loading of records that use a common schema, including Dublin Core, MARC XML, and EAD. As of 2010, Primo supports any structured XML format and can import this data with custom harvesting rules (Vaughan 2011a). Because repositories are such a common source of data, many vendors have experience with loading bepress, Dspace, ArchivalWare, and Fedora records. OCLC requires that local repositories be OAI-PMH compliant for harvesting, and it runs the records through the WorldCat Digital Collection Tool to crosswalk the metadata to MARC. Those records are then searchable

TEXTBOX 3.2.

QUESTIONS TO ANSWER TO DETERMINE THE TARGET AUDIENCE

1. Who are the prospective users of the service?
2. How will they be using the service?
3. What are the most important content sources for the targeted user group?
4. Will there be multiple, diverse targeted user groups who require custom profiles?

Questions for Vendors about System Content

Requesting a Content Analysis

1. Does the vendor have a partnership agreement with key publishers/content providers?
2. Are there expiration dates for these agreements?
3. What percentage of titles are covered?
4. Is the content included in the central index or otherwise?

Content Strengths/Exclusive Content

1. How much of the central index content is exclusive to the vendor/product?
2. What subject areas or material types are particularly well represented?
3. What e-book content is included?

Specialized Content

1. Can content not included in the central index or covered by a partnership be integrated?
2. How will it be presented and searched?

Depth of Metadata

1. Is indexing of A&I databases that are included in the product fully available for searching?
2. How much of the full-text abstracts or full-text documents are searchable?
3. How are records without much metadata or full-text content handled by relevancy ranking?

Suppression of Undesired Content?

1. Can some filters be turned on by default to suppress or default to certain content types?
2. How much of the central index content is mutually licensed?
3. Can some content sources be turned off or removed from the central index?

Multiple Profiles

1. Does the product allow the development of multiple profiles?
2. How can content on these profiles be customized?
3. Can the profiles have their own branding?

Local Content

1. Does the vendor have previous experience loading records from the source ILS/repository software?
2. How frequently can records be loaded, and how long does it take for new loads to process?
3. What formats are supported for loading, and what are the possible match points for bibliographic records?
4. What metadata from local records will be indexed, searchable, and displayed? How will these indexes translate to facets and limits?

in WorldCat generally. Inquire with the vendor about what types of records they support and have experience with loading. If there will need to be custom rules set up for harvesting and indexing the records, find out if there will be an extra fee involved and how long it will take to configure.

Normalization of records from these local sources for integration into the WSD service central index may not accommodate specialized fields or tags. Talk to the vendor about what metadata will be indexed and discoverable on the service and how it will be searched and presented.

Key Points

Making a good content match between the local and electronic holdings of a library and a WSD service is one of the most critical and difficult parts of the selection process. Because of the huge volume of records included in these services, it is nearly impossible to do a title-by-title comparison. Libraries should request a content analysis from the WSD service vendor in advance of purchase to get a report of coverage of key publishers and electronic content packages that the library subscribes to. Be sure to inquire about years of coverage and how long the agreement with the publisher/content provider will be in effect.

Some A&I services do not contribute their records directly to WSD services. Those that do are often exclusively held by just one of the services. WSD services may include the content direct from the publisher or from other services. Be aware that metadata from the source service, particularly indexing terms, may be different or not included.

Coverage of local content is also an important consideration. Inquire about the loading process for catalog records and other potential unique sources of data, such as digital repositories. Find out what metadata from these records will be discoverable in the service.

References

Daniels, Jeffrey, Laura Robinson, and Susan Wishnetsky. 2013. "Results of Web-Scale Discovery: Data, Discussions, and Decisions." *Serials Librarian* 64, no. 1: 81–87.

Grant, Carl. 2013. "Do They or Don't They: Ex Libris and EBSCO Information Services; Content-Neutrality and Content Silos." *Thoughts from Carl Grant.* Blog. June 13. http://thoughts.care-affiliates.com/2013/06/do-they-or-dont-they-ex-libris-ebsco_13.html.

Head, Alison J., and Michael B. Eisenberg. 2009. *Lessons Learned: How College Students Seek Information in the Digital Age.* Seattle: University of Washington, Information School. projectinfolit.org/pdfs/PIL_Fall2009_finalv_YR1_12_2009v2.pdf.

Hoeppner, Athena. 2012. "The Ins and Outs of Evaluating Web Scale Discovery Services." *Computers in Libraries* 32, no. 3: 7–10, 38–40.

Kelley, Michael. 2012. "Stakeholders Strive to Define Standards for Web-Scale Discovery Systems." *Library Journal* (October 11). http://www.thedigitalshift.com/2012/10/discovery/coming-into-focus-web-scale-discovery-services-face-growing-need-for-best-practices/.

Luther, Judy, and Maureen C. Kelly. 2011. "The Next Generation of Discovery." *Library Journal* 136, no. 5: 66–71. http://www.libraryjournal.com/lj/home/889250-264/the_next_generation_of_discovery.html.csp.

ProQuest. 2013. "ProQuest's Interoperable Platforms Reduce Barriers to E-book Discovery." http://www.proquest.com/en-US/aboutus/pressroom/13/20130409.shtml.

Vaughan, Jason. 2011a. "Primo Central." *Library Technology Reports* 47, no. 1: 39–47.

———. 2011b. "Questions to Consider." *Library Technology Reports* 47, no. 1: 54–59.

CHAPTER 4

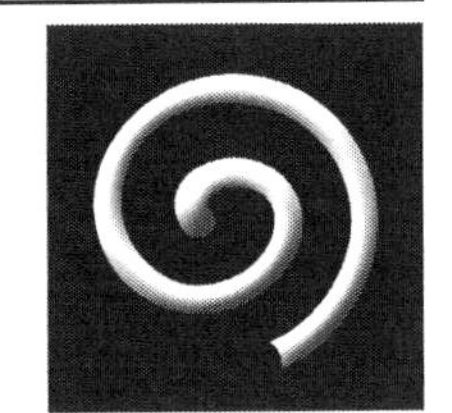

Evaluating the Discovery Layer

IN THIS CHAPTER

- ▷ Defining the Discovery Layer
- ▷ Exploring Searching Features
- ▷ Assessing Record Display
- ▷ Examining Tools to Manage Searches and Retrieval
- ▷ Evaluating Social Media and Other Enhanced Content Features

Defining the Discovery Layer

WHILE THE CONTENT AVAILABLE FOR SEARCHING is a critical factor in selecting a web-scale discovery (WSD) service, the options for searching, displaying, and winnowing retrieval are just as important. As discussed in chapter 1, the discovery layer provides this structure as the search interface. On WSD services, the volumes of content being searched are massive, and searching is frequently across the full-text of documents. While abstract and indexing (A&I) databases provide highly structured indexing to allow precision retrieval, WSD services that pull content from many diverse sources use other means for users to retrieve useful results. Relevancy ranking, search facets, content filters, sorting and de-duping options, and recommender services are tools available on most of these services to target the most relevant content. Once a good retrieval set is acquired, the display of records and the tools to manage retrieval are also an important part of creating a quality search environment. This chapter presents discovery layer features that should be considered when evaluating WSD services.

- Relevancy ranking
- Facets and filters
- "Did you mean?" and spell-check features
- Advanced search options

Relevancy Ranking

Finely tuned relevancy-ranking algorithms are as important to successful searching in the WSD environment as they are to web search engines such as Google and Bing. They vary across systems, are generally highly proprietary (as in the search engine world), and are tailored to the core content in the service's central index. Factors that are typically part of a relevancy ranking formula include the following:

- Currency
- Number of search term occurrences in the document
- Field of occurrence (can vary by type of publication)
- Proximity of search terms

Ask the vendor for specifics of how relevancy ranking works on the system. Ask what fields are most heavily weighted and the importance of the aforementioned factors.

Another critical selection factor is the degree to which relevancy ranking can be customized by the subscriber. Can currency be more or less of a factor? Can certain fields be targeted, such as material type (peer-reviewed materials on academic systems)? Can local collections such as catalog records have heavier weighting so that they appear further up in search results?

Systems that search across a high percentage of full-text documents and heavily weigh term occurrence may bury records with just a bibliographic citation and limited metadata. Inquire about how these items are handled.

Facets and Filters

Facets and filters allow users to winnow large search retrieval sets to those that are the most useful. Available facets and filters typically appear in a left-hand column on the search results display, with filters listed first. The order can usually be determined by the library.

Filters are usually toggled on and off by clicking on a checkbox or radio button. Filters that most services feature include the following:

- Publication date (often as a sliding gadget)
- Full-text availability
- Availability in local collections
- Source type (academic journals, book, newspaper article)

Facets are typically derived from the metadata fields included in the central index. As noted by Hoeppner (2012, 38), the different services have unique facets that emphasize their content strengths:

> WCL has several facets useful for books that are based on standard MARC fields, such as audience, genre, and geographical area. . . . EDS has a range of potential facets coming from its abstract and index databases. PCI lets the implementing library choose any field to use as a facet.

Most services include facets for the following:

- Language
- Content provider
- Publication
- Author
- Subject terms

Since the facets that appear are dependent on the metadata fields available in the content, they are frequently dynamic. For example, services that include a lot of business content resources may provide facets for company name or industry type, which appear when a business inquiry is executed and retrieves content from these sources. Services that have scientific and medical data may generate facets for age or gender. Though the presence of these less common but highly specified facets may seem like a useful feature, they have their limitations. Applying a facet for a metadata type that does not occur across all the content sources being searched can remove all the hits from those content sources—for example,

- Academic Search Premier and SportsDISCUS both have "Geographic Terms" metadata that display in a Geography facet.
    - CINAHL Plus does not have "Geographic Terms" to populate the Geography facet.
        - When searchers select a term in the Geography facet to narrow search results (e.g., *United States*), all records from CINAHL Plus drop out of the search results.

Because users were not aware that using highly targeted facets would remove many possibly relevant search results, Thompson and colleagues reported removing facet groups that were not common to all content sources, in their article on implementing EDS (Thompson, Obrig, and Abate 2013). This is sometimes problematic for language facets because some content sources do not include a language field or designation.

Summon recently introduced "Discipline-Scoped Search." Discipline metadata is assigned to central index content and appears as a facet group in search results. Fifty-nine disciplines are derived from several discipline classification sources, including Ulrich's.

Facets can usually be configured to just show a heading with the facet type that can be clicked on to show possible selections or open to show a limited set of selections that can be expanded. An illustration of this is in "Customizing Facets and Filters" (chapter 8). Usually, the number of results that would match that selection is shown in parentheses.

When investigating facet and filter options on a WSD service, inquire how customizable they are on the system. What facet groups and filters can be turned on or off? Can some filters be set as defaults? Some libraries choose to turn on the full-text-only filter so that users initially retrieve only records with access to full text. If desired, users then have the option to uncheck the filter and see all results. Libraries purchasing Summon can set the default for the filter to eliminate newspaper content. Setting similar defaults may help to increase initial search result relevancy.

"Did You Mean?" and Spell Check Features

Many WSD services will provide search suggestions or alternate search terms if a search results in no hits. EDS has a drop-down that displays as the user is typing his or her search that shows common inquiries that begin the same way that the user can then select. On Primo, the library can determine when the "Did you mean?" prompt appears dependent on the number of hits retrieved (e.g., 50 or fewer) (Vaughan 2011a). Primo also provides a facet category for Suggested New Searches. Summon has an option to execute the search beyond the library's collection if there is no retrieval, as well as displaying alternate spellings or searches to try.

Inquire about what options are available to prevent a dead-end search: What spell-check and "Did you mean?" features exist on the system? Are there other suggestions for expanding the search or trying alternate terms?

Advanced Search Options

Most libraries will opt to put a simple keyword search box front and center to emulate Google and other search engines, but library staff and more sophisticated users may desire the extra functionality that comes from a more complex search interface. All the services provide an advanced search feature that allows simple Boolean searching (AND, OR, NOT) on multiple fields, and application of multiple limits/filters.

Options to aid in finding specific known items are usually included in the advanced search screen. For example, EDS allows input of a specific publication date and journal title here. Users can also search by ISBN/ISSN. Summon allows limitation to particular content types in advanced search, and WorldCat Discovery Service allows targeting by Audience (e.g., Juvenile).

Most of these services do not support a traditional browse function or call number searching out of the box (with Primo being the exception). Phrase searching and proximity operators are frequently supported, but it is often difficult to find information about this type of searching in the default search interfaces.

Assessing Record Display Features

- Sorting and de-duping
- Brief (search result) record view
- Full record view

Sorting and De-duping

On most WSD systems, the default sort for search result sets is by relevancy ranking to display the most relevant results at the top of the hit list. All four allow this default to be changed after the search is launched and an initial set of hits is displayed. Alternate sorting options are generally limited by date ascending or descending, and the selection to change usually appears as a drop-down at the top of the brief record display. Primo, which is very customizable, allows custom sort options to be developed. Libraries can choose to allow sorting on author, title, or any other fields.

Because WSD systems draw records from so many content sources, there are frequently duplicate records retrieved in a search. The same citation may be available in multiple content sources. Duplicate detection and elimination is a feature of all these systems. Inquire about how this is achieved. Are certain content sources favored over others for display? Does the system display the record with the most metadata? The most sophisticated option is the creation of a merged or super record that aggregates all the metadata from the differing sources into one record. This is usually available only for the content sources included in the central index.

Brief (Search Result) Record View

The main search results view page on WSD services has limited real estate for the display of records. Generally, the search query box appears at the top; facets and filters display along the left-hand side of the screen; and options for continuing the search in other sources or managing results can sometimes appear in a third column to the right. Results themselves display in a list in either the right-hand or middle column. Figure 4.1 shows the search results screen in WorldCat Discovery Service.

Libraries can typically set the default for the number of records that will appear on a page. This is often set for 10, but depending on the length of the records available on this screen, it can be set for more. The number of records to display on a page is also frequently a drop-down menu option that can be adjusted by the searcher.

How the actual result records are displayed is often customizable, allowing libraries to determine how much of the record will be available for users to view and decide if they want to see the full records or full text. The fields that display on the brief records page are set to a default that can often be changed by the searcher if desired. On EDS, there are options for a very brief record that shows just author, title, source, and publisher data or a view that also includes indexing terms and an abstract if available. EDS can also be configured to display a preview of images from the record. Primo subscribers can select exactly what fields they would like to display; the view is completely customizable. On systems that have these options, libraries need to determine if it is of greater value to show more data up-front or keep screens cleaner and display more records per page.

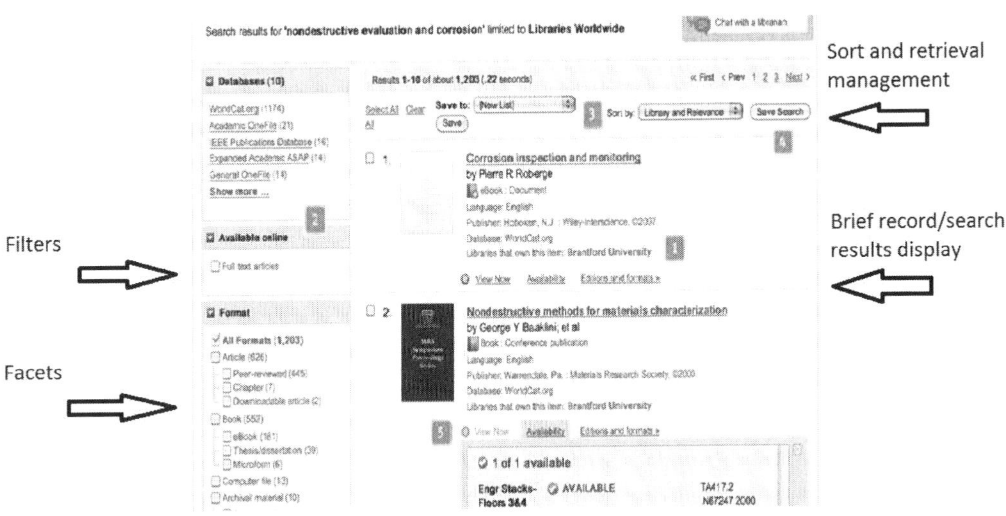

Figure 4.1. Search retrieval screen on WorldCat Discovery Service. *© 2014 OCLC Online Computer Library Center, Inc., used with OCLC's permission; WorldCat, WorldCat.org, and the WorldCat logo are registered trademarks/service marks of OCLC.*

Icons that visually inform users of what format is represented by the record usually display in the brief record. WSD systems supply stock icon images representing the formats (academic journal, book, news, etc.), and they are assigned on the basis of the metadata or source of the record. Some systems may allow the library to use a customized set of icons and control how they are assigned. For catalog items, cover art can be displayed for books and e-books that the library holds. Cover art can come from a content enrichment service that the library subscribes to (e.g., Syndetics) or a free source (e.g., Amazon, Google Books).

The brief record view also conveys if full text is available, and it presents users with options for retrieving and displaying it. Typically, a button is presented that takes users to the library's link resolver. On both EDS and Summon, there are direct links to the full text for mutually subscribed content. EDS often displays links to both PDF and HTML formats as SmartLinks in the search results.

For catalog records, the brief record view includes information about copies available at the library, as provided by screen scraping the OPAC or a direct search and display of data from the ILS via Z39.50. The brief record usually displays just the location and availability of the first copy. More detailed information about where other copies are located is usually viewable by clicking through to the full record view or the native OPAC interface, if that option is presented. WorldCat Discovery Service also presents options for viewing what specific editions and formats are available.

Full Record View

The full record view presents all the metadata available for the record and shows what the source of the record is (this is sometimes also displayed in the brief view). If not displayed on the brief view, searchers can see the abstract here if one is present. Cover art also displays here, if available for the record, and any other enrichment features for which the library subscribes. This can include table of contents data, Journal Citation Reports rankings and citation counts, review services, or user assigned tags. See the "Evaluating Social Media and Other Enhanced Content Features" later in this chapter for additional information about these services. Figure 4.2 displays a full record view from EDS.

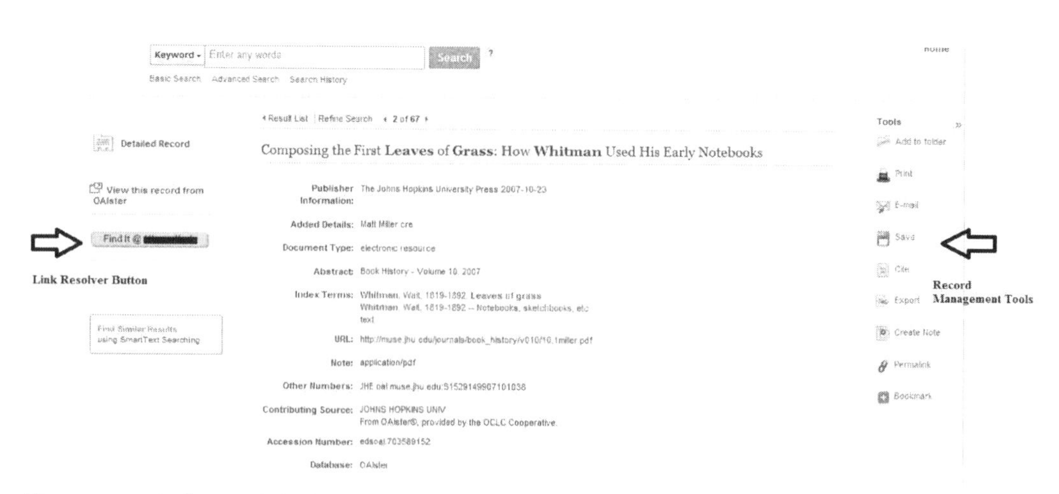

Figure 4.2. Full record display in EDS. *Courtesy of EBSCO Information Services.*

For bibliographic records that the library holds, a more detailed view displays, showing location and availability of all copies. As in the brief record view, this data comes from either a screen scrape of the OPAC or a Z39.50 query of the ILS. WorldCat Discovery Service goes a step further for these records, displaying holdings information for the local library and holdings for libraries that are geographically close or for other consortium members. A subscribing library can choose a custom group of libraries that it would like to include for display. Academic libraries that have consortial-type agreements with other local academics or special libraries could find this useful, and school libraries might want to display the holdings of local public libraries here.

As in the brief record view, direct links to full text appear in the full record view when available. If full text is not an option, there is usually a button to the library's link resolver or direct to document delivery services. Links to "Buy It" going to a third-party bookseller are sometimes an option, especially if a library uses jacket art from services such as Barnes and Noble or Amazon that request that Buy It options be enabled if their jacket art and other content are integrated.

On Summon, searchers can access the full record by hovering over the title of the brief record or by clicking the magnifying glass icon that appears in the upper-right-hand corner of each record; a pop-up window appears with the additional metadata, including subject terms and the abstract when available. This window is labeled "Preview." Clicking on the title takes the searcher directly to the link resolver or full text for ProQuest mutually subscribed content. Primo opens a window that expands on the brief results page to view the full record.

Examining Tools to Manage Searches and Records

- Saving searches and records
- Citing, exporting, and sharing

Saving Searches and Records

All the systems provide mechanisms for saving results to folders. These folders can be temporary or permanent. Temporary folders are saved only for the duration of the session. To permanently save a results folder, searchers generally need to set up an account on the service. WorldCat Discovery Service allows users who create accounts to save records to multiple "lists" that act like folders. Searchers can save to "Things I Recommend," "Things I Own," and "Things to Check Out" lists (Vaughan 2011b). Some of these lists can be made public and shared with other users, one of the many social networking features available on this system.

Search strategies can also be saved on WSD systems by creating a user account. For those who prefer not to create an account, creating a permalink for a search is available on some services. On EDS, this can be accessed by clicking the Alert/Save/Share button on the search results page and copying the URL that is presented in the box labeled "Use Permalink." EDS also provides permalinks for individual records. WorldCat Discovery Service similarly has a Permalink icon.

Other features offered for saving searches include setting up an alert via e-mail or RSS feed. Summon has an RSS feed button in the top-right-hand corner of the search results page. EDS, Primo, and WorldCat Discovery Service also have RSS feed capabilities.

Citing, Exporting, and Sharing

A popular feature of WSD systems is creating citations on the fly. Both EDS and Summon allow users to create a citation in a variety of common styles and copy it out. EDS's "Cite" button is on the Full Record view screen, while Summon's is on the full-text view page for ProQuest mutually subscribed content.

All four WSD services allow direct export of records to bibliographic citation management services, primarily RefWorks and EndNote. E-mailing, printing, and downloading citations is also typically available from the full record view screen and from folders or lists. On Primo, all these actions can be accessed by clicking on the Send To button.

Sharing to bookmarking services like Delicious or Digg is another common feature. Some also enable easy sharing to Facebook and Twitter accounts.

Evaluating Social Media and Other Enhanced Content Features

- Recommender services
- Social networking features
- Multilingual Support
- OPAC/library account services

Recommender Services

Availability and features of recommender services are an area where the four WSD products currently on the market distinguish themselves. EDS and WorldCat Discovery Service do not have recommender services (OCLC currently has an experimental API recommender service based on WorldCat data), while Summon and Primo have fairly sophisticated offerings. Primo has the bxArticle recommender service, which is derived from SFX data. Summon has a "More Like This" button on the full record view screen, as well as a Summon® Suggestions feature, which uses data from searches and full-text views on the system to offer database recommendations, related searches, and "Best Bets." More information on these services is available in the product profiles in chapter 2.

The importance of recommender services should be carefully considered, since there is a big difference in what is offered by the four services. Searchers who are used to recommender services in databases that they search may find them particularly useful or miss them if they are not present.

Social Networking Features

As with recommender services, there is significant divergence in the four services in how each provides tools for social networking. While most do allow bookmarking to services such as Delicious and sharing to Facebook and Twitter, the ability to tag and review items varies. Primo has a built-in interface for users to create tags, ratings, and reviews. Libraries have the option to approve user tags and reviews before they are made public. Likewise, WorldCat Discovery Service has integrated user tags and reviews, and libraries can choose to integrate reviews from WeRead. WorldCat Discovery Service also allows users to create profiles that include photos and interests. And as mentioned previously, WorldCat Discovery Service's lists features allows users to make lists public, such as "Things I Recommend" and "Things I Own."

Social networking is not a native feature of EDS, but libraries can choose to offer tags and reviews through the third-party service Chilifresh. Summon likewise provides tags and reviews through LibraryThing. As with recommender services, the importance of these features will vary from library to library.

Multilingual Support

The WSD services all provide alternate languages for screens for multiple languages. Summon has local support for over a dozen languages, including "simplified and traditional Chinese" (Vaughan 2011c). Primo has local language translation for over two dozen European and Asian languages. Users frequently have the option to reset the language on one of these systems under preferences settings, which can be saved for those who create an account. EDS also has full-text language translation.

OPAC/Library Account Services

Libraries that want to offer a true one-search experience and dispense with a separate OPAC altogether frequently face the obstacle of how to offer OPAC services. These services include "My Account" features, such as placing requests for holds and renewals, viewing checkouts and bills, and requesting address changes or renewing privileges. Many WSD systems require that users go back to the native OPAC interface for these services. Primo libraries that are on an Ex Libris ILS (Voyager, Aleph, or now Alma) can integrate these services directly into Primo. Similarly, libraries using OCLC's WorldShare Management system can access these services directly on WorldCat Discovery Service.

Summon is currently working toward offering these services directly in its interface without the need to go to the OPAC. This will make abandoning the OPAC altogether a possibility for Summon libraries down the road. Other options are integrating a third-party service such as Boopsie or Library Anywhere to provide OPAC My Account functions or using the API layer to develop calls to these services that display in the WSD service.

Key Points

The discovery layer of a WSD service is just as critical to the system's effectiveness as the underlying content. The discovery layer provides the search interface, options for refining retrieval to the most relevant records for the inquiry, and tools for viewing, saving, and sharing searches and retrieval. Though many of these features are common to the four services, each provides them in different ways. Recommender services, social networking services, and OPAC services do differ significantly, but the importance of these features will vary from library to library. The textbox contains a list of potential questions based on chapter content to ask vendors about discovery layer features.

TEXTBOX 4.1.

QUESTIONS FOR VENDORS ABOUT THE DISCOVERY LAYER

Relevancy Ranking

1. What fields are most heavily weighted?
2. To what degree does number of term occurrences in a record play in increasing relevancy? How are records with no full text and little metadata handled?
3. How much weighting does currency get, and can that be increased or decreased?
4. Can local library collections be boosted in search results?

Facets and Filters

1. How are facets generated?
2. Can customers turn facet groups on or off or develop custom facets?
3. Can some filters be set as defaults?

"Did You Mean?" and Spelling Checks

1. What happens when users retrieve no records on a search?
2. How and when are "Did you mean?" and spell-check correction prompts generated?

Advanced Search Options

1. What Boolean search features are enabled? Is phrase searching supported, and can proximity operators be used?
2. How is searching for specific items supported?
3. Is there a browsing function?

Record Sorting and De-duping

1. What sorting options are presented to users?
2. Can custom sorting options be developed?
3. How are duplicate records detected and culled?
4. Does the system have merged or super records?

Search Results Page/Brief Record View

1. Can the library control arrangement of the elements on the page (facets/search box/record management options)?
2. What are the options for the number of records displayed per page, and can this be set by the library or the user?

3. Can the fields of the record that display be changed by the user or customized?
4. How are the icons displaying record type assigned? Can this be changed, or can custom images be used?
5. How are links to the full record and full text presented? Is it easy to determine if full text is available?
6. What information about catalog record holdings is presented?
7. What record management tools are present on the search results page (save to folder, e-mail, etc.)?

Full Record View

1. What options are available for enhanced content? Can cover art, table of contents, or other data be included from free or subscription services (Syndetics, Google Books, Amazon, etc.)?
2. Can Buy This item buttons be displayed or suppressed?
3. What additional information about catalog record holdings display?
4. Can holdings of additional libraries (consortia members) display?
5. Are there links to the native catalog interface for catalog records?
6. Is a full record view page a separate page that can be linked to, or does this data display as a window within the search results page?

Saving Searches and Records

1. How can search results be saved? Can result folders or lists be saved permanently? Can these lists be e-mailed, downloaded, or shared with other users?
2. Can searchers easily generate permalinks for search strategies or individual records?
3. Can e-mail alerts for new search results or RSS feeds be set up to save and reexecute the search?

Citing and Exporting

1. Can users easily generate citations to copy out? How many different styles are available?
2. What bibliographic management services are supported for export (RefWorks, EndNote, Connotea)?
3. What services can users generate bookmarks to, and do these include popular social networking services, such as Facebook and Twitter?

Recommender Services

1. Does the service provide any Recommender features, such as recommending other databases to search or showing related records?
2. How are these recommendations generated?

(continued)

TEXTBOX 4.1. *Continued*

Social Networking Features

1. Does the service offer opportunities for users to tag, review, or rate items? Are these services part of the native interface or provided through a third-party service?
2. Can librarians mediate tags or reviews before they become public?
3. Can users share lists or items, either within the native interface or through integration with other social networking services?
4. Can users build profiles in their accounts with photos and interests that other users can view?

Multilingual Support

1. What other languages are offered for screens and helps information? Can users reset the language for a session?
2. Is full-text translation supported?

OPAC Services

1. Can users access library account information, such as number of checkouts or fines owed, without having to pass through to the native catalog interface?
2. Are renewing, place-hold, update-address, or renew-privileges services offered within the WSD service?
3. If these services are not built in, can they be introduced with a third-party service or developed through the API layer so that a separate catalog interface is no longer necessary?

References

Hoeppner, Athena. 2012. "The Ins and Outs of Evaluating Web Scale Discovery Services." *Computers in Libraries* 32, no. 3: 7–10, 38–40.

Thompson, JoLinda, Kathe Obrig, and Laura Abate. 2013. "Web-Scale Discovery in an Academic Health Sciences Library: Development and Implementation of the EBSCO Discovery Service." *Medical Reference Services Quarterly* 32, no. 1: 26–41.

Vaughan, Jason. 2011a. "Ex Libris Primo Central." *Library Technology Reports* 47, no. 1: 39–47.

———. 2011b. "OCLC WorldCat Local." *Library Technology Reports* 47 no. 1: 12–21.

———. 2011c. "Serials Solutions Summon." *Library Technology Reports* 47, no. 1: 22–29.

CHAPTER 5

Other Important Web-Scale Discovery Service Features and Functions

IN THIS CHAPTER

- ▷ Offering Mobile Platforms for Web-Scale Discovery Services
- ▷ Supporting Consortia and Multilibrary Systems
- ▷ Controlling Access and Rights Management
- ▷ Using API
- ▷ Tracking Usage
- ▷ Checking Accessibility Standard Compliance
- ▷ Accessing Technical Support and Training

Other Features and Functions to Consider When Purchasing a Web-Scale Discovery Service

CONTENT AND THE DISCOVERY LAYER WILL BE THE PRIMARY SELECTION factors when shopping for a WSD service. All things being equal or close, other features and functions should be considered in making evaluations. These include how mobile-friendly the service is, how well it supports consortia and multilibrary implementations (if required), and how the system handles authentication and rights management. On the administrative side, features for gathering and reporting statistics are important for assessing the success of the service and determining what may need further development. The ease of managing customization and configuration depends on the functionality of the administrative interface, the availability and openness of API for libraries that desire a very custom interface, and the quality of technical support during implementation and after. All of these are worth consideration when purchasing.

Offering Mobile Platforms for Web-Scale Discovery Services

Because of the number of options and amount of data displaying on search results screens in web-scale discovery (WSD) systems, having a mobile responsive interface is necessary for searching them on smaller devices. All of the vendors provide mobile-friendly platforms. EBSCO*host* products, including EDS, detect and adjust for devices other than full-size iPad tablets. On the iPad, it is the same screen presentation as on a desktop or laptop. Summon's screen adjustments on mobile include an even briefer brief record display that users have the ability to adjust using user preferences features. A Refine button at the top of the search results screens leads to facet and limiting options. Primo allows users searching the system on a laptop or desktop computer to send results to their phone or tablet via SMS. Both Primo and Summon allow the mobile version to be customized by the library.

Vendors are moving away from apps that are OS specific and have to be downloaded to responsive pages that detect mobile and adjust seamlessly using HTML 5. Devices generally need to be running a Java-based browser (e.g., Opera Mini) to be supported. OCLC decided to abandon the app that it developed with Boopsie (a third-party service offering mobile applications for library catalogs) for WorldCat Local when it rolled its new responsive interface out in the summer of 2011 (OCLC 2011). Some of the other services do still make apps available for Apple and Android users.

Supporting Consortia and Multilibrary Systems

In a consortium, large public library system, or multilibrary academic environment where libraries are sharing a system, the ability to both share data and differentiate among libraries is a priority. The WSD services frequently provide the ability for each individual library to have its own branding and build a custom interface. Primo claims to allow libraries in consortia to be as unified or separate as desired. Each library can "select its own settings for search options, user interface, calculation of item availability, and delivery options" according to Ex Libris's website (Ex Libris 2013).

The Ohio5 consortium reported the difficulty of building a single unified search environment that met the needs of all member libraries when it implemented Summon in 2010. Having individual instances for each school proved to be the best approach (Christel, Koehler, and Upfold 2012). Carlton and St. Olaf colleges also decided on separate instances of Summon due to complications from having separate licensure for almost all their electronic products. In their case, two other WSD vendors claimed to be capable of providing a joint license and instance, but ultimately they selected separate instances of Summon to fulfill other needs (Leebaw et al. 2013).

WorldCat Discovery Service allows libraries to assign relationships with other libraries in display of results. For consortia where libraries have individual integrated library systems and catalogs, this allows display of the holdings of the other libraries as long as they contribute their records to OCLC. Primo can search the indexes of other Primo sites if all participating libraries are Ex Libris ILS customers. Summon will work with consortia with disparate catalogs to present holdings in a single merged record. When a union catalog is loaded on EDS, users can search the holdings of multiple locations and limit to individual locations via facets. Separate profiles on EDS provide individual library branding and data settings.

Controlling Access and Rights Management

Because the majority of content on a WSD system is licensed, user authentication is a critical feature. The most common forms of authentication are supported across all the systems, including by IP range and proxy server (e.g., OCLC's EZproxy service). All also support single sign-on (SSO) services such as LDAP or Shibboleth.

Some libraries will want to offer guest (unauthenticated) access to the system. Primo allows the library to determine what a guest user can do up to the point of actually viewing full-text when log-in is required (Vaughan 2011a). If guest access is important, inquire at what point authentication is required and if unauthenticated users can search central index content and view search results. Unless the retrieved content is open access, viewing full text will always require authentication.

Rights management is usually provided through the library's link resolver. Most commercial link resolver products are supported by the four WSD vendors, though they often prefer to work with their own products, and each currently has a link resolver/rights management service. Ex Libris sells Primo and SFX. ProQuest sells Summon and 360Link. EBSCO sells EDS and LinkSource. OCLC's WorldCat Discovery Service has its own knowledge base and eSerials holdings service.

Close integration between link resolver/rights management and discovery product can help guarantee the best coverage and accessibility to mutually subscribed content. The University of North Florida reported dropping ProQuest's 360 Link product for EBSCO's LinkSource when it selected EDS to "reduce fingerpointing" when troubleshooting linking issues (Kucsak 2013). Even in situations where both products come from the same vendor, there can still be hurdles. Daniels et al. reported that the Summon implementation at Grand Valley State University where 360Link was used as the link resolver had issues linking to certain resources, including EBSCO database content (Daniels, Robinson, and Wishnetsky 2013).

Libraries using homegrown or customized link resolver solutions should do fact finding up-front to determine if their service will be fully supported. During Ohio5 Consortium's implementation of Summon, it discovered that its OLinks resolver would not work for certain types of content. It chose to implement Serials Solutions 360 Link product as part of its project (Christel, Koehler, and Upfold 2012).

There has been ongoing concern among content providers and library subscribers about bias in discovery service linking practices. Do WSD services link users to particular content providers' platforms more frequently because of the relationship between the two? The Open Discovery Initiative, a NISO working group developing standards for discovery systems, addresses this issue in its recently released draft for public comment, *Promoting Transparency in Discovery*. It calls for discovery services to enable libraries to "establish preferences regarding which platforms to present to users as link targets, and in what order of priority" (NISO Open Discovery Initiative Working Group 2013, 18). This not only helps to remove WSD/content provider biases but also allows the library to direct users to platforms that are potentially more reliable or more feature-rich.

Using API: Application Programming Interface

Libraries that desire a highly customized interface or that would like to export results or searches from the WSD direct to other applications will be able to achieve this through the system's API layer. All the WSD services were built with open architecture, making them open to web services queries. Primo provides read/write APIs to subscribers from the El Commons portal, which is maintained by its user community. Summon provides its API via the API Documentation Center and gives an authorization key to subscribers who wish to access it. OCLC has WorldCat Search API, which provides developer-level access to WorldCat. This is available to any library that has OCLC cataloging and First-Search (now WorldCat Discovery Service) subscriptions. EBSCO provides access to API for EDS to subscribers with comprehensive documentation and support.

Robust API layers allow libraries to take a WSD system's content and relevancy ranking to a different discovery layer if desired. Libraries may choose to use an open-source discovery layer, such as VuFind or Blacklight. This is discussed in more detail in "Examining Discovery Layer–Web-Scale Content Hybrids" (chapter 2). An API can also bring WSD content to learning or course management systems or other systems where library users might have need for their content. Inquire with the vendor what is possible with the API layer and how other customers have used it.

Being able to exploit API requires access to programmers with the appropriate skill sets (PHP, Java/JQuery, AJAX, RUBY, XML, among others). Inquire with the vendor what programming languages are required to work with their code. Some may be in the comfort zone for a librarian with a lot of web-authoring experience.

Tracking Usage

Once a system is implemented, usage information will be an important tool to gauge the appeal and effectiveness of the service. If the system does not have a flexible, easy-to-use tool that provides a variety of useful statistics, the subscribing library will not have the data to support and improve the search interface.

EDS has statistical reporting available through the administrative portal for EBSCO*host*. It offers the ability to download data directly to spreadsheet or e-mail reports in comma-delimited or XML format. Libraries can generate statistics for each profile if multiple profiles are configured. Reporting options include number of connections, number of searches, and number of full-text, abstract, or image views. The number of searches may not be a very accurate number, however. The search is counted for each EBSCO*host* resource that is included in the EDS instance being queried. This can greatly inflate the number. The system can generate queries for any time frame desired. Figure 5.1 illustrates the statistics reporter in the EDS administrative interface, and figure 5.2 is a sample output of statistics for a month on a system.

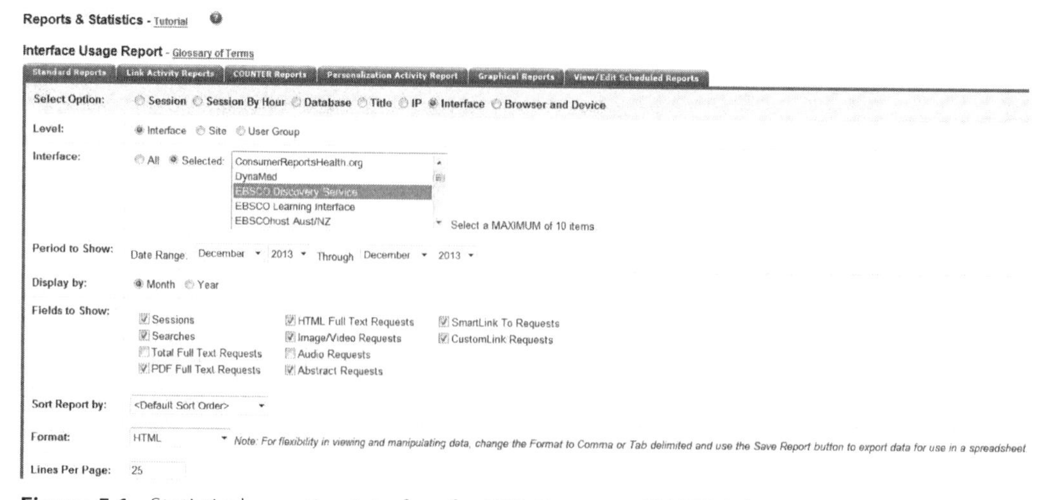

Figure 5.1. Statistical reporting interface for EDS. *Courtesy of EBSCO Information Services.*

Reports & Statistics

Interface Usage Report Site: Detail Level: Interface Period: December 2013

InterfaceID/Version	Year	Month	Sessions	Searches	Requests						
					Total Full Text	PDF Full Text	HTML Full Text	Image/Video	Abstract	Smart Link To	Custom Link
eds / live	2013	December	4191	724042	3578	3021	557	0	7759	712	2814

Figure 5.2. Monthly statistics sample from EDS. *Courtesy of EBSCO Information Services.*

Primo offers some additional data-gathering points that could be quite valuable. These include number of results per search, top searches with no results, and system response statistics (Vaughan 2011a). Summon Analytics administrative console provides several usage reports for subscribers—top search queries, usage breakdown by time of day, number of searches, and analysis by IP range, allowing the library to track where searchers are located. WorldCat Discovery Service includes statistics on holds placed and document delivery requests. Primo, Summon, and WorldCat Discovery Service also provide reporting on usage of facet and filter groups.

While EDS and Summon provide statistics generation and output via a web-based administrative module, both Primo and WorldCat Discovery Service require additional software to produce statistics. Primo relies on Google Analytics for usage metrics. Details for how to set collections up is documented in the Ex Libris El Commons Code Share site. WorldCat Discovery Services also uses Google Analytics but offers additional functionality through purchase of Adobe® Reports & Analaytics.® This web analytics program provides real-time reports on a number of data points, including facets usage, but does require some time to configure and learn to use. This makes it less user-friendly, but the added usage metrics available may make learning a new tool worth it.

Usage statistics is one of the focuses of the recent move toward standards for discovery services. The NISO Open Discovery Initiative now recommends that some basic usage and assessment data be collected and accessible for all discovery systems, and it promises that more complex metrics will be called for in the future. The November 2013 standards draft requests the following be provided to subscribers monthly:

- Total number of searches
- Total number of click-throughs to "full content" items
- Number of unique visitors
- Top 500 search queries
- Top 100 referring URLs (bringing searchers to the discovery service) (NISO Open Discovery Initiative Working Group 2013)

Additional information about the NISO ODI standards is in "Emerging Standards for Web-Scale Discovery" (chapter 12).

Checking Accessibility Standard Compliance

Public, government, and academic libraries at publicly funded institutions may need services to meet certain web accessibility standards or adhere to Section 508 of the Rehabilitation Act, which addresses accessibility for websites and web services to accommodate visual, auditory, physical, speech, cognitive, and neurological disabilities. Only federal website agencies are compelled to comply with Section 508; however, the guidelines may be used to help determine if a site is accessible. More information about Section 508 can be found at http://www.buyaccessible.gov/beaccessible.

Some technology and information services vendors have posted accessibility compliance information to the government's Buy Accessible website (http://buyaccessible.net/VARC/), but none of the web-scale discovery vendors are included. EBSCO does maintain a webpage with accessibility information for all EBSCO interfaces at http://support.epnet.com/knowledge_base/detail.php?id=5755. Inquire with the other vendors what accessibility standards their services currently meet and what their target is for meeting those that they do not presently comply with. Required accessibility standards should be included in the RFP document if an RFP process is required for purchase (see "Stepping through the Selection Process," chapter 6).

Accessing Technical Support and Training

While WSD services are sometimes billed by vendors as potentially "out of the box" services, there is always some basic configuration and customization needed. For libraries who have specialty subject environments, who have a complicated consortial or multi-library environment, or who otherwise desire a high level of customization, the need will be intensive. The difference between a smooth implementation and a bumpy one frequently depends on the knowledge, skills, and attentiveness of the vendor's technical support personnel.

Prospective buyers should inquire about the services that are provided and the capability of the staff supplying them. Will there be an assigned implementation specialist who will guide the buyer through configuration? If a multilibrary purchase, will the same person be supporting all the libraries? Will this individual continue to be the point person for support postimplementation? If the vendor has a staff member pegged for implementation support, find out how long the individual has been supporting the product and managing implementations. It is particularly helpful to have someone who has brought up similar sites previously and can be proactive in guiding a new buyer through decision points.

All the WSD services provide an administrative interface or module that customers can use to configure and brand their sites. EDS uses the same administrative module as that provided for EBSCO*host* databases, thereby reducing the learning curve for libraries that are already EBSCO*host* customers. It provides basic branding, the ability to designate what EBSCO*host* resources are included in content, facet and filter selection, defaults for sorting and record views, and screen configuration (one-, two-, or three-column options). Libraries can also turn on or off chat support, designate links to other services, add helps documentation, and generate search box widgets. Summon Customizer is a web-based administrative tool that provides branding options, including incorporation of custom-style sheets and widgets from outside services (Vaughan 2011b). Prospective customers should request a walk through the administrative console or module prior to making a purchase decision to find out how easy it is to navigate and what options for customization are readily available without requiring a service request.

The vendors frequently make support videos and tutorials available via their websites. Find out if more formal training opportunities exist and if there is comprehensive documentation of the product available for customers. OCLC keeps links to extensive WorldCat Discovery Service support documentation on a single webpage at http://www.oclc.org/support/services/discovery/documentation.en.html. Also inquire if they periodically provide updates on new functions or features beyond just a press release or announcements to user Listservs.

Ongoing support after implementation is just as important as the guidance provided initially. All four services offer 24/7 support, and support requests can be generated by phone, e-mail, or website. Ask vendors how long it typically takes to resolve a request and if there are any methods to track progress. Another helpful support feature is a user group where customers can share information about the product and offer support and guidance. Ask if an associated Listserv or other forum for sharing information is available and how active it is.

TEXTBOX 5.1.

QUESTIONS FOR VENDORS ABOUT OTHER FEATURES AND FUNCTIONS

Mobile Platform

1. Is the mobile platform app based or automatically detected and delivered when users are on a mobile device?
2. What devices/OS are supported?
3. Are all the search, display, and record management features of the service available in the mobile version?
4. Can the mobile version be at all customized?

Support for Consortia

1. Can libraries on a multilibrary system build individual instances through profiles or other means with unique branding, content, and search settings?
2. Can holdings of all consortia members be shown in item holdings details?
3. Can multiple locations be searched simultaneously?

Authentication and Link Resolver Support

1. What authentication technologies are supported?
2. Is guest/unauthenticated access an option?
3. What can unauthenticated users search and view? Can this be determined by the library?
4. What commercial link resolver products can be integrated? Will a competitor link resolver provide the same level of access to mutually subscribed content?
5. Can the subscriber to some degree dictate link target preferences and order of priority?

API

1. What can be done with open API and web services?
2. How is API made available and supported?
3. What programming languages and technical knowledge do staff need to exploit APIs?

(continued)

TEXTBOX 5.1. *Continued*

ADA/Section 508 Compliance

1. What accessibility standards does the service currently meet? Is there a target for meeting standards if not currently compliant?

Technical Support and Training

1. Who will manage the implementation? If a multilibrary installation, will the same staff be assigned to all libraries?
2. How long have support staff worked for the vendor? Have they done similar implementations in the past?
3. What can be managed by the service's administrative module? Is a demo of the module possible?
4. What training resources are available? Is comprehensive documentation accessible?
5. How are software updates and new features communicated to customers?
6. What hours is customer support available, and how can support queries be submitted?
7. Is there an active user group and associated Listserv or other forum for sharing information?

Key Points

Though less important than content and discovery layer features, the presence and functionality of mobile platforms, support for consortia or multilibrary environments, effectiveness of rights management, extent of available statistics and usage reporting, and the user friendliness of the administrative interface are all items that should be explored and considered when selecting a web-scale discovery service. Libraries that desire a very custom application or who wish to export data from the WSD to other systems or services will want to inquire about availability and openness of the API layer. Also important is the quality and accessibility of technical support from the vendor during and after implementation. The textbox contains a list of potential questions based on chapter content to ask vendors about these other features and functions.

References

Christel, Mark, Jacob Koehler, and Michael Upfold. 2012. "Implementing a Discovery Layer in a Consortial Environment." In *Planning and Implementing Resource Discovery Tools in Academic Libraries*, edited by Mary Pagliero Popp and Diane Dallis, 407–18. Hershey, PA: IGI Global.

Daniels, Jeffrey, Laura Robinson, and Susan Wishnetsky. 2013. "Results of Web-Scale Discovery: Data, Discussions, and Decisions." *Serials Librarian* 64, no. 1: 81–87.

Ex Libris. 2013. "Primo for Your Library." http://www.exlibrisgroup.com/category/PrimoForYourLibrary.

Kucsak, Michael. 2013. "Delivering the Goods." *Web-Scale Discovery Services: Transforming Access to Library Resources.* NISO virtual conference. November 20. http://www.niso.org/news/events/2013/virtual/discovery/#slides.

Leebaw, Danya, Brian Conlan, Kasia Gonnerman, Sarah Johnston, and Christina Sinkler-Miller. 2013. "Improving Library Resource Discovery: Exploring the Possibilities of VuFind and Web-Scale Discovery." *Journal of Web Librarianship* 7, no. 2: 154–89.

NISO Open Discovery Initiative Working Group. 2013. *Promoting Transparency in Discovery: A Recommended Practice of the National Information Standards Organization.* Draft. Baltimore, MD: National Information Standards Organization. October 15.

OCLC. 2011. "WorldCat Local Mobile Now in Production." News release. June 17. http://www.oclc.org/news/releases/2011/201134.en.html.

Vaughan, Jason. 2011a. "Ex Libris Primo Central." *Library Technology Reports* 47, no. 1: 39–47.

———. 2011b. "Serials Solutions Summon." *Library Technology Reports* 47, no. 1: 22–29.

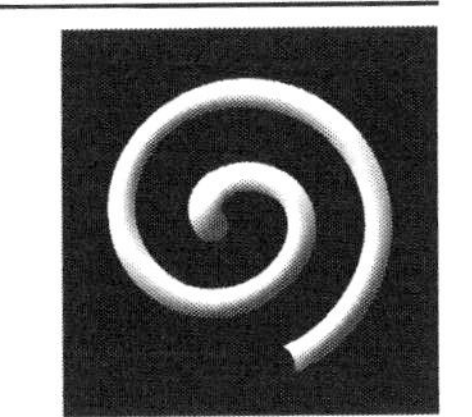

CHAPTER 6

Selecting and Purchasing a Web-Scale Discovery Service

IN THIS CHAPTER

- ▷ Stepping through the Selection Process
- ▷ Trialing Web-Scale Discovery Services
- ▷ Negotiating a Price That Fits

Stepping through the Selection Process

Prioritizing the Library's Discovery Needs

BEFORE TALKING TO VENDORS, the purchaser should have at least a well-defined checklist of required features and functionality. The three prior chapters can be used to help develop a checklist and specific questions to ask vendors. The table in the appendix can also be used as a starting point. It is likely that no system will include everything that is desired in a WSD system for a particular library. Establishing "must have" features and content and prioritizing the rest are recommended to identify a system that is a best match for a library's needs. The table in the appendix includes a scoring system (having a required element results in the product getting a 3 for that feature, not having it a 0), which provides a tool to prioritize and an evaluative measure for scoring one product over another.

Considering other products that the library has that will interact with a potential WSD service is another important factor. If the library has many ProQuest databases and uses 360 Link and ProQuest's electronic resource management systems, Summon may be a good choice because of the amount of mutually subscribed content and the ability of the link resolver to make as much of it optimally available as possible. A library with many

EBSCO*host* databases may find EDS to be a good match for content and the familiarity of the search interface for users. Ex Libris ILS customers may want the close integration of the integrated library system and catalog services that Primo could offer. Libraries that use OCLC document delivery management products and have FirstSearch subscriptions could find a best match in WorldCat Discovery Service.

Unique needs of the user population should be considered when ranking features and functionality. A community of scientific researchers could find recommender services, such as those found in Summon and Primo, to be extremely useful and something that they are used to having in other search and discovery products, such as SciVerse and PubMed. In public library settings, social networking features, such as those found in WorldCat Discovery Service, may be high priority.

The sophistication of technical support staff and time available for development are other factors that should be carefully considered. Although all the WSD products require some degree of configuration and customization, some are more "out of the box" friendly than others. Consider the ease of the administrative interface, especially for doing basic setup, such as branding and integrating the catalog and link resolver. On the flip side, a library with an entrepreneurial bent and dedicated programming staff may prefer a product with a well-developed and documented API layer.

Affordability will also frequently play a role in whittling down the possibilities. Potential subscribers should have a range in mind when speaking to vendors. The section at the end of the chapter, "Negotiating a Price That Fits," provides tips on how vendors determine pricing and ways to get to a workable number.

In summary, consider the following in prioritizing your library's discovery needs:

- Determine "must have" features and functions
- Consider the interface with key products, including link resolvers and ILS
- Take into account the unique needs of the user population
- Decide how much customization is desired or feasible
- Factor in affordability

Assembling an RFP

In some environments, a formal request for proposal (RFP) process will be required to make a purchase. RFPs have their advantages and disadvantages. On the one hand, they create a level playing field for all prospective products by establishing objective, measurable criteria for evaluation (Clegg and Montgomery 2006). On the other, the time and effort required to pull together a thorough RFP document and get vendors to respond with written proposals can slow down and complicate the process.

An RFP will require a thorough review and documentation of the environment, detailed requirements of the product that must be met or addressed, and a method of scoring responses to these requirements. Bidders must be given instructions on how to respond to the RFP and submit questions; they also must be informed of how the selection decision will be made and what the timeline is for the evaluation and decision process. Freivalds and Lush (2012) discuss how a formal RFP process was used at Penn State University to purchase a discovery service (Freivalds and Lush 2012). Along with assembling the RFP document and making it available for bid, they formed an evaluation team, brought vendors in for demonstrations, and checked references as part of the process. One of their recommended take-aways was making the scoring guidelines clearer, especially for staff who were not as familiar with discovery systems.

If an RFP is not required, a less formal "needs" document can be helpful in establishing and documenting evaluation criteria and required functionality for systems to be considered. The Bridge Discovery Tool Taskforce, which selected a web-scale discovery product for Carleton and St. Olaf colleges, developed a detailed Statement of Need and Requirements to aid in the evaluation process (Leebaw et al. 2013). Consider utilizing the following steps of the RFP process, even if an RFP is not required:

- Assemble a needs document
- Create a scoring method for evaluating each product
- Invite vendors for product demonstrations
- Contact references

The following sections include some of the structure and advantages of following an RFP process without requiring a formal document and responses. If an RFP is required, work to turn it into a method to make the purchasing process structured, thorough, and fair.

Determining Decision Makers

Introducing a discovery system like a WSD service has a major impact on staff, users, and the library's budget. Because it is such a large and consequential purchase, selection is rarely left to just one or a few decision makers. In medium to large and multilibrary environments, a selection committee is typically designated to drive the process. The committee should include representation from IT support and web services staff, electronic resources specialists, reference and instructional services staff, technical services staff with a deep knowledge of the library's metadata and integrated library system, and

TEXTBOX 6.1.

LIBRARY STAFF MEMBERS TO INVOLVE IN THE WSD SELECTION TEAM

- *Electronic resources support specialists* with knowledge of authentication methods and link resolver services
- *Cataloging/metadata specialists* with a deep knowledge of the library's local record structure and metadata
- *Web services staff* who will construct search widgets, configure branding, and fit the services into the library's web presence
- *Reference and instructional services staff* who know the searching needs and capabilities of library users
- *Collection development specialists* who know the library's collection holdings in depth
- *IT support staff* who can help integrate the service with existing systems and know the requirements of local network, software, and browser configurations

collection development librarians who know the library's collection holdings in depth. If the library has previously explored or implemented a federated search or next-generation catalog system, staff involved in research and implementation of those systems should be included, as their expertise and experience will be valuable.

Involving other staff who will work closely with the product in the selection decision has advantages. Reference and instructional staff often have the best knowledge of the needs of library users, and they frequently have strong opinions one way or another about the need for a discovery system. Having them participate in the selection process brings this wealth of information to the table and helps demonstrate to them why a discovery system is a worthwhile service to offer. The Bridge Discovery Tool Task Force identified library staff as key stakeholders early on and involved them in an open and inclusive selection process (Leebaw et al. 2013). On the flip side, having many staff voicing conflicting opinions can bog down the process if it is too open-ended. In a recent survey of 15 academic libraries that implemented discovery systems, 60% of large- and medium-sized institutions had difficulty reaching staff consensus in the product purchased (Metz-Wiseman et al. 2012). When involving staff beyond the selection committee, provide structured means for soliciting input and feedback, including surveys, focus groups, or participation in usability testing.

Some libraries will choose to involve end users directly in the selection process, while others will be opposed to exposing users to a service that has not been optimally configured and customized for their use. End users can be given access to trial sites and can participate in focus groups or interviews with library staff involved in selection. Usability studies are another way to solicit detailed feedback on a product from the user perspective. More information on setting up trials is in this chapter, and chapter 10 discusses conducting usability tests.

Scheduling Vendor Demos

One of the first steps in the shopping process is typically inviting vendors to demonstrate and talk about the product to staff or the selection committee. An efficient way to do this step is to attend a professional conference (e.g., ALA) where many of the vendors are present in the exhibit hall. Scheduling a meeting with the vendor ahead of time and outside of when the exhibit hall will experience maximum traffic is recommended. It can still be challenging to have an in-depth demonstration in the exhibit hall environment, but it may provide enough information to eliminate an obviously incompatible system.

Scheduling an on-site demo will be easier to arrange when there is a previous relationship with the vendor or if the library is in a major metropolitan area. If on-site is not possible, all the vendors have the capacity to set up a webinar. A webinar provides the option for staff to participate from their individual workstations or meet in a conference room for group viewing. This can be advantageous, particularly for multilibrary environments, where staff are scattered in different locations.

Providing the vendor with some specific system features to demonstrate or a list of questions in advance can help the presenter be better prepared. If the vendor does not have a previous relationship with the library, sending other pertinent information about the local environment or having an introductory phone call can help them tailor the demonstration to local needs and interests.

Vendors will include searches tested ahead of time to get good results when doing a demonstration. Ask them to do some searches off the cuff that are typical of what library users will be searching to see how the system does in a "real world" environment. Request test searches that will prompt spell-check and "Did you mean?" features to see how effective they are outside the vendor-canned demo examples.

If mobile platforms are important, ask for a way to see the service on several devices to test the appearance and functionality. Also recommended is taking a quick look at the administrative interface to see what can be easily configured and customized and how user-friendly it is.

After the demo, get the group who viewed it together to share reactions and feedback. It is recommended to run this meeting like a focus group with preplanned questions and a method for recording responses and further questions for the vendor. A follow-up phone call with the vendor is recommended to pass along thanks and to get answers to any questions that came up during the demonstration that the presenter was not able to answer immediately or afterward in the feedback meeting with staff.

Calling References

Contacting references is usually a requirement of an RFP process. Even if no RFP is required, talking to other libraries that have already implemented a product provides important information about the implementation process and the quality of vendor support. Ask the vendor for a list of all sites that it has implemented in the last year and are of similar size and type to the purchasing library, to be contacted for a reference. If just two or three references are requested, chances are that the sites included on the list from the vendor will have had a smooth implementation experience and mostly positive things to say.

At minimum, ask references about the implementation experience, including whether the product was delivered on time, the experience and expertise of support staff, how easy the administrative interface was to work with, and what implementation tasks were done by the vendor and which were left to library staff. Also ask about the quality of ongoing support, the reliability of the service, and the level of satisfaction with the service once released to users. A suggested final question is "Will you be renewing your subscription for next year and, if not, why?"

If the number of questions is extensive, ask the reference contact if the questions can be sent in advance. This gives them the option to answer in writing or have more prepared answers for a telephone interview. If the reference contact opts for written response, make an appointment to discuss responses and follow up on any areas of concern.

Trialing Web-Scale Discovery Services

Establishing If a Trial Is Worth Running

When WSD services first came to the market, there was such an urgency to get them into libraries that most vendors were willing to spend extensive time and effort setting up highly customized free trials for any library interested in purchase. That urgency is a thing of the past, so trials that will be a good representation of a fully configured implementation are trickier to negotiate with vendors. Large sites, consortia, or sites that are in a segment of the market into which the vendor would like to further expand will have more success negotiating a trial that will be a good representation of a fully configured system.

When requesting a trial, ask how much configuration the vendor will be willing to do in advance. If it does not include integration of local collections, such as the catalog and the library's link resolver, it will not be a good representation of the implemented service. Even if the vendor is willing to do that work for a free trial, there is a host of further customizations that could be done that will not be possible in the limited sphere of a trial.

A trial will provide a means to get a sense of how friendly the search interface is, how well default relevancy ranking works, what content is included in the central index, and how the tools for managing and saving searches and search results function. A trial will also provide insight into what will require further work beyond an out-of-the-box installation to make the service viable for the library. This allows the trialing library to assemble a list of items that would need to be addressed in a fully implemented system and find out if these adjustments and customizations are feasible. This may be enough to make a trial worth pursuing, even if it is not representational of a fully configured system.

Setting up a trial will be like a mini-implementation. Technical services and electronic resources staff involved in selection will be required to go through many of the steps involved in a full implementation to configure the library's link resolver and load local records. Basic branding is sometimes allowed to give the trialing library an idea of branding options. The selection team will also need to determine how the trial will be made available; publicize it to staff, users, or both; and construct evaluation tools to get needed data on the service's performance. Some of the time and effort involved in setting up the trial can be applied to the system if purchased, as the vendor will usually save those configurations and apply them to the live site.

Deciding Who Should Participate

One of the biggest questions about a trial for many libraries will be whether to involve library users directly. Exposing users to a trial version of a system is a double-edged sword. It can provide excellent insight into what features and functions of the system are less than user-friendly, and it will help reveal areas that need further attention down the road if the service is purchased. On the downside, exposing users to a service that needs a lot of additional work can turn them off to the service before it has a chance to be developed. Some of these risks can be minimized if trials are available to users in a controlled environment, such as usability tests or by inviting a select group of users to try it and participate in a focus group. This can help minimize frustration and ensure that users fully understand that the system is merely under consideration and will require further refinement before it becomes generally available if purchased. It also helps ensure that the library gets useful feedback.

Some of the same risks will also come into play if library staff members who are less knowledgeable or enthusiastic about web-scale discovery participate in trials. Providing some instruction and orientation to web-scale discovery in advance will help. Also asking for specific feedback in the form of a survey or questionnaire can make the responses staff members provide more useful and easily evaluative. This can be particularly valuable if several systems are trialed and a standard set of questions is used.

Conducting Trials and Trial Alternatives

Areas to examine in a trial are available facets and limits and how they function, effectiveness of "Did you mean?" and spell-checker features, the information available in brief and full record views, and sorting and record management options. To see all the available facets, Belford (2014) suggests doing an extremely broad search ("history") to see the facet groups generated. Searching known records and spot-checking brief and full record display will reveal labels, item details, and what tags and subfields display for catalog records. Pay attention to how limits function, such as language limits (do certain content sources drop out completely when applied?). Relevancy ranking is also important to assess as it is an area that subscribers tend to have limited control over. If the library has narrowed the field to two viable candidate systems, scheduling side-by-side trials can be particularly revealing. It will mean double the work up-front, but being able to run searches simultaneously in both systems and compare retrieval is extremely helpful in assessing content and relevancy-ranking strengths and weaknesses for each.

In cases where a trial is not possible or the vendor is unwilling to preintegrate a trial with the library's local collections, using services that are already implemented at similar libraries for some test searching is a possible alternative. Vendors often publish lists of subscribers on their websites, and Marshall Breeding's *Library Technology Guides* website's Discovery Services page (http://www.librarytechnology.org/discovery.pl) provides a list

TEXTBOX 6.2.

SEARCHES TO RUN AND THINGS TO LOOK FOR IN TRIALS

- Try very broad searches to display all available facets. Are there facets that are potentially important to users that do not display?
- Run searches on known items to test ease and accuracy of retrieval.
- Search for catalog items to see if they appear high in search results or are buried in article/full-text content.
- Deliberately search with misspellings or typos to test "Did you mean?" and spell-checker functions
- How relevant are the items that appear in the top-20 search hits? How current? Does a particular content source seem to dominate results content?
- Test limit and facet applications—can multiple facets be selected? Is it clear to searchers that limits are applied when entering new search terms or limits?
- Is phrase searching possible, and how well does it work?
- Is browse searching available if important?
- Can stop words be searched literally in quotations?
- What MARC fields and subfields display and appear to be searchable for catalog records?
- How are fields and subfields labeled in brief and full record display?
- Are search terms highlighted in search results? Where are they occurring?
- Is it apparent when full text is available, and is click-through to full text easy? Do users have options to download as PDF or HTML?
- Can permalinks for records and searches be generated on the fly? How do they work?
- How easy is it to save records to lists, manage folders, and generate and export citations?

of subscribers for each product. Many implemented sites allow guest searching, although unauthorized searchers will be unable to click through to full text. Still, this provides a method to launch test searches and see available search, sorting, and output options. If this method is used, keep in mind that each library will bring in its own unique content and that there may have been customizations done that affect relevancy ranking, available facets, and appearance and content in record views.

Negotiating a Price That Fits

Pricing Models for WSD Systems

As with many database packages, there is no "one size fits all" pricing for WSD systems. Cost usually depends on a number of local factors. These commonly include the size of the user population, the number of local records that will be loaded, the number of FTE staff, and in the case of Summon, the degrees granted by the institution for academic customers.

The pricing model is also similar to databases in that it is more like a subscription and less like an integrated library system or a service that requires local hardware that is purchased with a large up-front commitment of cash and then supported with annual maintenance fees. Subscription fees are generally inclusive, covering support, software enhancements and updates, and loading and integration of local records. Since WSD systems are almost exclusively hosted, the subscription includes hosting and platform support as well. The only system that can be locally hosted is Primo, which may affect subscription costs.

Sometimes development and integration of unusual content sources can influence support and pricing. For example, if EBSCO has to program an integrated resource for EDS because the code has not been developed for another library previously, there will be additional programming costs.

The subscription cost will be fairly similar in subsequent years, allowing for inflation, which makes the system easy to budget for year to year. This subscription model will, in theory, allow for a move to a different vendor if a library is unhappy with the service, since there is not a large outlay of cash out front. However, libraries do need to consider the labor and time involved in making a switch and the impact to users of switching systems up too frequently.

Making a WSD System Fit the Budget

The following can help mitigate the costs of a WSD system:

- Multiyear contracts
- Bundling with other products and services from the vendor
- Canceling subscriptions or other products that are no longer needed with a WSD (federated search, next gen, or classic catalog)
- Purchasing as part of a consortium or becoming an add-on to another library's subscription

Since the WSD system will be an entirely new service for most libraries, finding the funding to support it is often a challenge. A number of strategies can be considered if none of the initial vendor quotes will work for the current budget. One of the easiest is to consider a multiyear contract, which will usually include discounts. The downside is being unable to switch without penalty if service begins to degrade or another product becomes more attractive. As stated in the previous section on pricing, making the time and resource investment in configuring, marketing, and supporting one of these systems is rarely justifiable for something that will only be kept for a year. If multiyear is considered, it is not recommended to commit to more than three years, as the landscape is changing quickly.

Sometimes another product can be supplanted by a WSD service, freeing up funds to help pay for it. The most obvious of these is if the library already subscribes to a federated search service. There may also be databases whose content is largely covered in a WSD central index that the library could consider canceling. More radical is the possibility of eliminating the native catalog interface if account features such as managing renewals and holds can be supplied via the WSD service.

Subscribing to other services from the same vendor may help to bring down costs. WorldCat Discovery Service is now the search interface for libraries that are FirstSearch subscribers, and it may not cost much more to add content from other mutually subscribed sources like EBSCO. If the library has link resolver, electronic resource management, or ILS products all from the same vendor, it may be possible to negotiate a volume deal.

Sharing a WSD service with another library or consortium members will lower the price quite significantly. As discussed in the section on multilibrary implementations (chapter 5), separate profiles can usually be established, allowing each library to have separate branding, unique content profiles, and default settings. Each library should carefully explore if having separate link resolver products and authentication control can be supported in a multilibrary implementation. The purchasing process will be more complex and require compromise from the participating libraries, but being able to afford to put something in place may make these concessions worthwhile. Once the service has demonstrated its value, it may be possible to justify the expense of a single library implementation down the road.

Key Points

The purchasing process for a WSD system will depend on the library environment. For some libraries, a formal RFP process will be required. An RFP will help ensure that systems are thoroughly investigated and that the selection process is fair and transparent. If an RFP is not required, many elements of the process, such as developing a needs document and contacting references, can still be incorporated to ensure a similar outcome.

Evaluation and selection will be team driven in most libraries. The process may or may not include members of the user community. If they are involved in evaluation, a structured and guided exposure to the candidate systems is recommended. Trials can be set up to provide a closer look and to run real-world searches to see how well certain elements of the system perform. However, trials will show only the default, out-of-the-box version of the service. They can allow the evaluation team to develop a list of items that must be improved or resolved in a fully implemented service. Searching on WSD services implemented at other libraries that allow guest access is an alternative to setting up trials.

Pricing, like the purchase process, will be highly dependent on the environment. Pricing formulas consider number of FTEs, student populations, and even degree-granting status in some cases for academics. To help make a system fit tight budgets, libraries can consider multiyear contracts, eliminating other products that may be less important with a WSD system in place, or participating in a multilibrary implementation.

References

Belford, Rebecca. 2014. "Evaluating Library Discovery Tools through a Music Lens." *Library Resources and Technical Services* 58, no. 1: 49–72.

Clegg, Helen, and Susan Montgomery. 2006. "How to Write an RFP for Information Products." *Information Outlook* 10, no. 6: 23–31.

Freivalds, Dace, and Binky Lush. 2012. "Thinking Inside the Grid: Selecting a Discovery System through the RFP Process." In *Planning and Implementing Resource Discovery Tools in Academic Libraries*, edited by Mary Pagliero Popp and Diane Dallis, 104–21. Hershey, PA: IGI Global.

Leebaw, Danya, Brian Conlan, Kasia Gonnerman, Sarah Johnston, and Christina Sinkler-Miller. 2013. "Improving Library Resource Discovery: Exploring the Possibilities of VuFind and Web-Scale Discovery." *Journal of Web Librarianship* 7, no. 2: 154–89.

Metz-Wiseman, Monica, Melanie Griffin, Carol Ann Borchert, and Deborah Henry. 2012. "Best Practices for Selecting the Best Fit." In *Planning and Implementing Resource Discovery Tools in Academic Libraries*, edited by Mary Pagliero Popp and Diane Dallis, 77–89. Hershey, PA: IGI Global.

CHAPTER 7

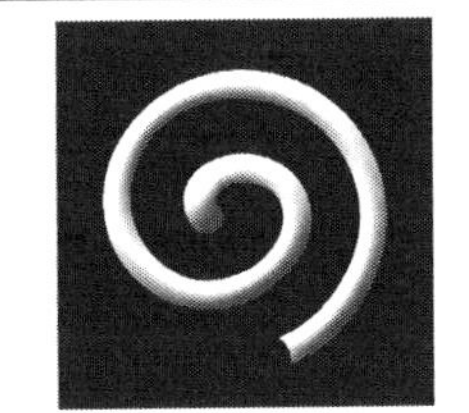

Configuring System Content Integration and Customization for Local Needs

IN THIS CHAPTER

- ▷ Loading Catalog Records and Records from Other Local Sources
- ▷ Connecting Other Content Sources
- ▷ Tailoring Central Index Content
- ▷ Configuring Link Resolvers

Loading Catalog Records and Records from Other Local Sources

ONE OF THE MOST LABOR-INTENSIVE AND CRITICAL TASKS in configuring a WSD system for the local environment is bringing local content in and making it findable. Local content can include local catalog records, repository or archival records, and records from locally created and maintained databases. The following addresses loading catalog records that follow MARC standards and loading other record types, keeping these records updated, and including them in a shared central index. Setting up live calls to the local catalog or ILS to bring in current status and location information is also discussed.

Loading MARC Bibliographic Records from the Local Integrated Library System

Because bibliographic data is typically stored in MARC record format, loading catalog records from the local integrated library system is usually straightforward. If loading MARC records from one of the large, established ILS systems, such as Millennium/Sierra, Unicorn/Symphony, Voyager, Notis, and Aleph, the vendors have all loaded records from these systems previously, and the preload work is usually as easy as filling out a standard questionnaire. Here is some of the information that the vendor will require to configure the records for loading and display:

Fields for match on the bibliographic record (title level)—This is usually set for the OCLC # (001 or 035 tag), ISBN/ISSN (020/022 tags), or occasionally the 907a tag (b# location for Innovative systems). This allows matching and overlay for subsequent updating record loads.

Item/holdings information and display—The tag that includes item information is frequently the 945 or 907 in the MARC record. Subfields within this tag include location and material-type information that will need to be mapped to values displayed in the system. The vendor will need to know where to find this information and how to display it. Figure 7.1 shows a sample map.

Holdings Information	MARC field & subfield
Call Number	945 subfield a
Call Number Additional Information (eg, volume or copy number)	945 subfield c for volume 945 subfield g for copy
Library Location	945 subfield l
Shelf Location (if coded separately from library location)	None
Barcode or copy identifier	945 subfield i

This sample table gives the WSD vendor the tags and subfields to find critical item information in the MARC file of catalog records.

Location Code	Copy Display	Facet Display	Delimeter Display
3av	Audiovisual Third Floor	Audiovisual Third Floor	Audiovisual Third Floor
3hist	Historical Collection	Historical Collection	Historical Collection
3net	Internet	Internet	Internet
3new	New Book Shelf	New Book Shelf	New Book Shelf
3offs	Off-site Storage	Off-site Storage	Off-site Storage
3ons	On-site Journal Storage	On-site Journal Storage	On-site Journal Storage
3pavl	Print Available	Print Available	Print Available
3rfcs	Reference Case	Reference Case	Reference Case
3rf	Reference First Floor	Reference First Floor	Reference First Floor
3rsrv	Reserves	Reserves	Reserves
3stx	Book Stacks	Book Stacks	Book Stacks
3stff	Staff Collection	Staff Collection	Staff Collection

This sample table provides labeling for the WSD vendor to use for location codes supplied in the catalog records. Note how there could be different labels for their display for copy info in the brief and full record view, for display within a facet group, or as a delimeter

Figure 7.1. Sample mapping for item information extraction and display.

Permalink syntax to search for a specific catalog record by URL—The system can be set up to link into the catalog and display the catalog record by matching on the call number, OCLC number, or ISBN/ISSN. A sample permalink for a SirsiDynix eLibrary OPAC matching on ISBN looks like this: http://catalog.library.edu/uhtbin/cgisirsi/0/0/0/5?searchdata1=0443079412{020}. Contact the ILS vendor for assistance.

Determining tags that populate fields and facets—Some systems allow libraries to determine exactly how the tags and subfields will populate certain fields for indexing and populate facet groups. The vendor may have a default mapping that can be adjusted for local practice. Libraries with collections that have specialized tags (music, archives, cartographic, etc.) should pay close attention to how these tags are mapped to facets and indexed. See figure 7.2 for an example of mappings for author and genre.

If a library is not on one of the more common ILS systems or cannot output records in MARC format, there will be more work to do with the WSD service vendor to provide records in a standardized format that can be loaded and indexed (see "Loading Repository Records or Other Record Types" in this chapter).

Once the questionnaire and data mappings are provided, the library is typically given an FTP site and destination to send a full file of records. Most ILS systems include a reporting mechanism to pull together the group of records to send and a utility to export the file in MARC format, including the item information. Once the file is FTP'd to the WSD vendor's server, the initial load and indexing can take a week to several weeks to complete.

For libraries that choose WorldCat Discovery Service, no record load may be needed if the only local source is catalog records and the library includes all holdings in OCLC's WorldCat. A reclamation process is recommended before going live to make sure local holdings in WorldCat are up to date. Reclamations are usually free and involve sending a full MARC record file to OCLC once for record matching. Records must include an OCLC number for match. Any records that do not match are returned to the library to determine if they should remain in the WorldCat database or not.

Libraries that are on an Ex Libris integrated library system and select Primo will run an internal process to regularly update catalog records. Similarly, libraries that are on Innovative or SirsiDynix ILS systems will not need to load records if they select the EDS hybrid products for Encore or Enterprise, which incorporate EDS content directly into the Encore and Enterprise discovery layers.

At the University of North Florida, the library opted to skip the ILS altogether and load electronic serial records from the vendor direct to EDS. The library determined there was not a need to manage these items in the ILS, since this was already being done in the ERMS system (Kucsak 2013). This may be a practice that more libraries adopt with the increase in electronic-only content. Libraries that wish to do this should closely examine the metadata in the electronic resource records and provide mappings as would be done for records coming from the catalog.

Index/Facet Group	Tags and Subfields to Include
Author	100 $u; 110 $u; 111 $u; 600 $u; 610 $u; 700 $u; 710 $u; 711 $u; 800 $a; 810 $a;
Genre	600 $v; 610 $v; 611 $v; 630 $v; 648 $v; 650 $v; 651 $v; 655 $a $v

Figure 7.2. Sample mapping for indexing and facet groups.

TEXTBOX 7.1.

RECOMMENDED FURTHER READING FOR LIBRARIES WITH SPECIAL COLLECTIONS

Belford, Rachel. 2014. "Evaluating Library Discovery through a Music Lens." *Library Resources and Technical Services* 58, no. 1: 49–72.

Belford takes a detailed look at MARC tags and subfields that feed discovery layer indexes, with special consideration for the unique metadata associated with music formats. The article will help music librarians make decisions about the best discovery options, but it will also help libraries with other types of special collections consider how their own unique metadata is handled.

Configuring Live Calls for Catalog Record Location and Status

Once records are initially loaded, the WSD service will usually be configured to make a connection to the integrated library system to pull in live status and location information for the items attached to the bibliographic record. The two methods utilized are screen scraping of the OPAC (a method of incorporating data directly from a webpage) or establishing a Z39.50 connection to the ILS to retrieve the data. The latter is preferred if the ILS has a Z39.50 port that can be open to the WSD service because it is more precise. The ILS vendor can provide the information that the WSD vendor requires to establish the connection. This includes the domain, the database type, the port, and the username and password if required.

For libraries behind a firewall, it may be necessary to add the vendor's IPs to those allowed to connect to the Z39.50 port. This will need to be coordinated with the local IT office if the ILS is hosted on-site or with the ILS vendor if the ILS is hosted by it.

Loading Repository Records or Other Record Types

The WSD vendors can generally load most local databases with records in standard formats, such as Dublin Core, EAD, and structured XML. For most vendors, any metadata meeting OAI-PMH standards is workable. Vendors commonly have experience loading from the most popular archival and repository software, including AchivalWare, Contentdm, Dspace, Fedora, and Digital Commons/bepress.

Local records will be normalized to some degree to fit the standards of the central index. For example, OCLC will load any OAI-PMH-compliant source and will crosswalk it to MARC before loading to WorldCat Discovery Service. Some fields, such as title and publication date, may be required to be present in the local records to create a record in the central index. Collections that have specialized record fields that are critical to maintain should be discussed with the vendor to make sure that they can be exposed and indexed for discovery. Creating facet categories for these fields may also be desired.

As with the catalog records, if the vendor has previously loaded records from digital repository software being used, the easier the loading process will be. Those using unusual or homegrown software will need to work closely with the vendor to properly map fields to their corresponding counterparts in the central index.

Keeping Local Records Updated

If local catalog records or other local collections require initial loading, they will need to be updated on a regular basis through the same process. The frequency and method of update will depend to a large extent on the collection being updated. Large libraries that are making substantial changes to the local database on a daily basis will want to send daily updates to reflect these changes. Smaller libraries that add just a few records a week may opt for weekly or biweekly update.

Libraries with large collections will also find it more manageable to routinely send just update files of new records and deletes rather than the entire database. A smaller library could opt to send the full load of records every time to ensure that the updates do not get out of sync with the local database. Large libraries sending just update files routinely should consider sending a full load every three to six months to be certain that all new records are included and deleted records removed.

For those doing a daily load, it makes sense to work with the local ILS vendor and WSD vendor to develop an automated process in the form of a script or reports that generate the updates and then send them via FTP to the designated server. An API could also enable an automated process.

Contributing Records to the Common Central Index

In the cases of both Summon and WorldCat Discovery Service, records from the catalog, repositories, or other local sources that are loaded become available in the central index content and can potentially be searched by all Summon customers or, for WorldCat Discovery Service, in WorldCat generally. Summon searchers are defaulted to searching only content available in the library but have the option to "Add results beyond your library's collections" and search the catalog and repository records of other customers. In 2010, that was 50 academic library collections, but the customer base has grown significantly since then (Vaughan 2011). WorldCat Discovery Service customers have the entire WorldCat system holdings available for search.

Connecting Other Content Sources

Some local content may consist of unique commercial databases that are important to the user community but not available in the central index. Niche databases or content from competing vendors can frequently be included without becoming part of the central index. This generally means that the WSD vendor will work to develop a federated search connection to the content source. For example, Primo uses Primo Deep Search, an API tool, and Metalib, the company's federated search service, to make connections to pull in content not included in the central index.

In EDS, "integrated search" sources display to the right-hand side of the search results display screen, and users have the option to check the box next to them to include results from that source with the search. Results run separately but are integrated into the rest of the retrieval set. An illustration displaying the integrated resource configured for an academic health sciences library is shown in figure 7.3.

If the content source has already been developed in this way by a previous customer, the source can frequently be made available at no cost. However, if a library is the first to want to include it, there is usually a fee for the programming hours required to create the federated search connector, or "pipe" as it is sometimes called.

A frequent problem with federated search is that when the remote content source has a change in database structure, the programming will require updating. Libraries including federated search sources will need to check their status regularly to make sure that they are still functioning as expected.

Libraries are also cautioned about including databases with only a few licenses or seats available. Displaying them prominently as an option in the service may result in WSD service users tying up the few available licenses, preventing access through the native interface.

Tailoring Central Index Content

While many libraries will have the objective of making as much content as possible available to users to search through a WSD service, others may be concerned about exposing users to volumes of content that is largely of no interest or inappropriate. This may be particularly the case for special libraries and school libraries.

Limiting or blocking this content can be achieved through several methods. Some of the WSD services, including EDS and WorldCat Discovery Service, allow subscribers to do some selection of which database and content sources that feed the central index are included or excluded. For EDS, this selection can be done through the administrative portal. In situations where content is actively selected for inclusion or exclusion, the settings should be reviewed regularly, as the vendors are continuously adding new databases and content sources.

Many of the services also allow default limits to be set to block certain content types. For example, Summon has a limit to exclude newspaper content. This can be turned on by default with the searcher having the option to remove it if news sources are desired. EDS allows all searches to default to "Available in the Library," which displays only local records and central index records for which the library has mutually subscribed content. This default can help ensure that users are seeing content that is selected by librarians. If

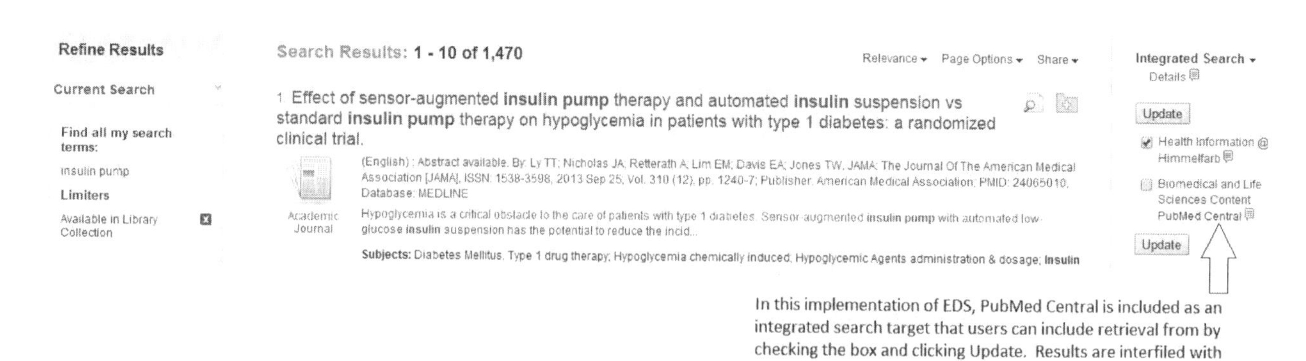

Figure 7.3. Including PubMed Central as an integrated resource in EDS. *Courtesy of EBSCO Information Services and Himmelfarb Health Sciences Library, George Washington University, Washington, DC.*

defaults like these are enabled, they should be clearly visible to searchers so that they are aware of the content limits and how to remove them.

Another content-tailoring method is to boost relevancy of certain content that is more likely to be desired by users. This is available if the vendor allows the library to customize relevancy ranking to some degree. For example, Primo allows libraries the ability to customize relevancy algorithms, including refining boosting metrics, which can push certain record fields higher in relevancy. A medical library may want to boost more current content, while an academic library may want to boost content from academic or peer-reviewed sources.

Configuring Link Resolvers

Link resolver services are required for users to link through to full text of most items retrieved in a WSD search. The four commercially available WSD services all accommodate use of the common link resolver products on the market (SFX, 360 Link, LinkSource, etc.), though maximum compatibility will often be realized in situations where the link resolver and WSD service come from the same vendor. Part of the configuration process will be providing the local link resolver's settings, including the base URL.

WorldCat Discovery subscribers automatically get free access to the WorldCat Knowledge Base (KB) for libraries. Libraries that maintain holdings in WorldCat and the WorldCat KB receive access to a built-in OpenURL resolver in WorldCat Discovery. Libraries that already have a link resolver from another provider can enable use of that resolver from WorldCat Discovery. Usage of the KB enables the View Now feature, which provides direct links to full text from the brief record in search results. EDS also includes the ability to link directly to full text from the brief record view without the link resolver for full-text content that the library subscribes to via EBSCO through its SmartLinks.

Because the ability to seamlessly click through to full text is such a critical function of web-scale discovery, testing should be done prior to releasing the service to library users to ensure that the link resolver is functioning as expected. Broken links were such a problem for Montana State University when the library first implemented Summon, that they became dubbed "full-text red herrings" by staff and resulted in lack of librarian buy-in to the service (Babbit, Foster, and Rossmann 2012). Some changes to the resolver configuration may be required. UTSA Libraries looked closely at performance of the link resolver after implementing Summon and reprioritized the list of databases from which the resolver retrieved full text to the most reliable sources. They also clarified language and adjusted positioning of text directing users to different options (Kemp 2012).

Nonstandard and homegrown link resolver solutions may not be fully supported. This should be addressed with the WSD vendor prior to purchase so that there are no surprises during implementation. As mentioned in a previous chapter, Ohio5 Consortium discovered that its in-house OLinks resolver did not function correctly for some content types when Summon was implemented. The solution ended up being a hasty move to 360 Links (Christel, Koehler, and Upfold 2012).

Libraries will sometimes supply button images to embed in the brief and full record views in the WSD service to connect to the link resolver for full-text or document delivery options. These buttons should be attention getting, readable, and very clear in their language so that it is readily apparent to users how to get to full text.

TEXTBOX 7.2.

COMMON CONTENT CONFIGURATION TASKS

Local Record Import and Updating

1. Complete vendor questionnaire supplying match field(s) for records, item record field mappings, and permalink structure for records.
2. Produce a MARC file for bibliographic records to include in the WSD service; records from other local sources should be output in a standard format, such as Dublin Core, EAD, or structured XML.
3. Records are FTP'd to the vendor's servers using credentials supplied by the vendor. Initial loading can take a week to several weeks.
4. Establish a schedule for updating records (adding new and deletes) dependent on the library's needs for currency. An automated process should be established for daily or more frequent updates.
5. Send the vendor local Z39.50 connection information (domain, port, and database) to retrieve live location and status information for catalog records representing physical objects.

Connecting Other Content Sources

1. Determine if the vendor supports integrating content via federated search or other means for content that cannot be supplied via the central index but is critical for local users.
2. Check licenses for databases to be included as integrated sources to make sure that there are adequate simultaneous seats/connections allowed.
3. For content sources that have not been previously configured by the vendor, request pricing for creating the connector or "pipe."
4. Test the resource after it becomes available and on a regular basis afterward to ensure that changes on the content vendor's side do not break the connector.

Tailoring Central Index Content

1. If the vendor allows selection of databases or content sources to include in central index content for a particular implementation, review the list of options and select those to be eliminated, if any. This will need to be reviewed regularly as the vendor adds new databases and content sources.
2. Determine if any default limits, such as removal of newspaper content or "Available in Library Collection" should be applied. Make sure users can see the limits and remove them if desired.
3. Make adjustments in relevancy rankings to boost particular record types or field contents if allowed by the vendor.

Configuring Link Resolvers

1. Provide settings for the local link resolver via the initial configuration questionnaire or administrative portal.
2. Test resolver performance and make adjustments to prioritization of sources or language used to direct users to full text.
3. If supplying buttons for the link resolver, make sure that they are attention getting and legible.

Key Points

Content configuration on web-scale discovery systems involves the work that needs to be done to make as much of the content desired for inclusion in the service available for retrieval and display of full-text content when available. Delivering records from local sources that the library would like to make available is frequently the most time-consuming and intensive of these tasks. Local records usually come from the catalog/OPAC but could also include archival, repository, or other home grown database contents. The library will need to supply records in a standard format (MARC, Dublin Core, OAI-PMH compliant XML) and mapping of fields for search and display. The WSD vendor will frequently normalize records to fit the central index formatting and indexing. Records with unique fields should receive special attention to ensure that this data remains discoverable.

Local content can also include unusual databases or other content sources that are critical to library users but not included in central index content. These sources can commonly be included utilizing federated search or web services queries. The subscriber may need to pay for development of the connector for sources that have not been configured by other customers previously.

Besides including local content, some refining of the delivered central index content may also be desired. Libraries may be able to actively select resources to include or exclude from the central index for their implementation. Other methods of tailoring content include applying search defaults and customizing relevancy ranking.

Finally, configuring the library's link resolver is critical to ensuring that users can click easily through to full-text content. Most commercially available link resolver products are supported by all four WSD services. Testing should be done in advance of releasing the system to make sure that link through to resources is reliable and clear to users.

References

Babbit, Elizabeth P., Amy Foster, and Doralyn Rossmann. 2012. "Implementation of Resource Discovery: Lessons Learned." In *Planning and Implementing Resource Discovery Tools in Academic Libraries*, edited by Mary Pagliero Popp and Diane Dallis, 598–607. Hershey, PA: IGI Global.

Christel, Mark, Jacob Koehler, and Michael Upfold. 2012. "Implementing a Discovery Layer in a Consortial Environment." In *Planning and Implementing Resource Discovery Tools in Academic Libraries*, edited by Mary Pagliero Popp and Diane Dallis, 407–18. Hershey, PA: IGI Global.

Kemp, Jan. 2012. "Does Web-Scale Discovery Make a Difference? Changes in Collections Use after Implementing Summon." In *Planning and Implementing Resource Discovery Tools in Academic Libraries*, edited by Mary Pagliero Popp and Diane Dallis, 456–68. Hershey, PA: IGI Global.

Kucsak, Michael. 2013. "Delivering the Goods." *Web-Scale Discovery Services: Transforming Access to Library Resources.* NISO virtual conference. November 20. http://www.niso.org/news/events/2013/virtual/discovery/#slides.

Vaughan, Jason. 2011. "Serials Solutions Summon." *Library Technology Reports* 47, no. 1: 22–29.

CHAPTER 8

Configuring and Branding the Discovery Layer

IN THIS CHAPTER

Branding and Customizing the System's Appearance

TWO COMMON WAYS TO CUSTOMIZE a WSD service's appearance for the local environment is through the use of branding and cascading style sheets. Branding clearly labels the system as belonging uniquely to the institution. Cascading style sheets provide a means to incorporate the colors, fonts, and design of the local webpages in the service.

Branding is routinely done and usually easy to accomplish. Most vendors provide an easy way to plug an institutional logo onto the main search screen. Once a name for the system is established (see "Marketing the Service" discussion in chapter 9), a logo or graphic that incorporates it could also be developed for use here.

Typically, there are also label areas above or below the main search box that can be customized through the administrative portal to display the institution's or service's name. Footer space can sometimes be altered via the administrative portal to include the institution name and address and, frequently, a link back to the library's main page. See the following section for more information on other links or menu options commonly available.

Cascading style sheets, or CSS, can frequently be incorporated into a WSD service to customize the background colors, font types, and other design elements. This can effectively integrate the WSD service into the institution's web presence and make it recognizable as belonging to the institution. The Michiana Academic Library Consortium uses three levels of CSS for its member libraries to customize Primo: The first layer provides a base appearance; the second provides consortium identification; and a third allows designation of elements unique to the institution (Bales and Dehmlow 2012). The use of more advanced branding like this is usually not supported directly by the vendors. The library will need to have staff capable of web design work to incorporate CSS into the site.

Tailoring Menu Bars, Links, and Labels

WSD services frequently include a menu bar that appears at the top of all pages or a customizable area to add links to other pages and services. Sometimes these include elements that are delivered by the vendor. For example, EDS has fixed elements, including log-in to the My Account services and access to the Preferences menu, and Primo has links to Help and Language settings. Alternately, the library may be able to customize all.

Elements that libraries frequently include are listed in the textbox. These range from the library's chat reference service to links to other content services, such as an A-to-Z list of e-journals. Though it can be tempting to put as much as possible that might be useful to users here, libraries that are configuring a system should consider the "noise" factor of making too many items available on these menus.

TEXTBOX 8.1.

COMMONLY INCLUDED MENU BAR ELEMENTS

"Ask a Librarian" chat services

"A-Z Journals" lists

Subject database access

Search assist or FAQ for the service

Library homepage link

Library catalog

Feedback or "Found an Issue?" form

A link back to the library's homepage is a fairly essential element that should be provided somewhere on all search pages. An easy link to assistance, such as a chat service, is also recommended for inclusion. Furthermore, there should be a prominent link for initiating a new search that does not carry any of the limits or defaults from the previous search.

Each service uses default labels that are often customizable. If a label used does not seem clear, investigation of the administrative portal may provide a way to easily change it. For example, the Integrated Resource label that EDS uses for the extra sources that can be brought in via federated search is likely not going to be understandable to many users and can be relabeled. Milner Library at Illinois State University opted to change this label to "Additional Results," which the implementation team thought would be more intuitive to users (Foster and Williams 2012). If there is not an easy way to change a label through the administrative portal, inquire with the vendor to see if it is a change that can be made by the support team.

Constructing Search Boxes and Widgets

The search box for a WSD service is not limited to its own isolated webpage. All the vendors allow libraries to construct search boxes and place them wherever access to the service is desired on the library's homepage, even in other services or applications. Search boxes can be placed in any service that allows an embedded search widget, allowing the library to put them where the users are already.

> The single search box can be placed in course management applications such as Blackboard, or, ideally, into the student's workflow, wherever that may be. As Jennifer Duvernay at Arizona State University (ASU), an early installation of Summon, notes, "We can't wait for the students to come to us; we have to go to them, embedding the search where they are working." (Luther and Kelly 2011)

The default search box presentation for these services is usually to a simple keyword search that mimics the search box on other search engine sites, but this can often be customized. The library may prefer to put a search interface with Advanced Search features, which allow Boolean combinations of terms and limits up-front instead. If the basic keyword search presentation is the one used, there is sometimes an option for a drop-down menu or radio buttons that allows users to switch from the keyword index to title or author search. A link to the Advanced Search interface can also be incorporated to make users aware of the option. Primo provides a Browse Search option. Figure 8.1 is a sample search box for a WorldCat Discovery Service instance.

Creating search boxes can be done with HTML code, or vendors often make the code available in the form of a search widget constructor, which allows easy configuration of a custom search box with minimum or no coding skills required. ProQuest and EBSCO both provide search widgets that can be customized in this way for their search services. OCLC also has an easy-to-use search box builder for WorldCat Discovery Service and a five-minute tutorial on how to use it. The search widget builders can sometimes allow more advanced customizations, including limits to particular formats or content. This can provide a means to build focused search boxes for particular needs. For example, a search widget with defaults to American history sources could be embedded in a webpage for a school's history department. See the final section in this chapter, "Creating Specialized Profiles," for more information.

Example search box:

Figure 8.1. WorldCat Discovery Service sample search box. *© 2014 OCLC Online Computer Library Center, Inc., used with OCLC's permission; WorldCat, WorldCat.org, and the WorldCat logo are registered trademarks/service marks of OCLC.*

How to present the search box for the WSD service can have a significant impact on design of the library's homepage. Will it become the primary search interface, displacing the library's OPAC or prominent display of database search options? Fortunately, these services provide a lot of flexibility in how they are incorporated. Libraries that wish to put the WSD service front and center can do so, or the search box can be included in a more balanced approach. Research has shown that providing a prominent single search box option can greatly increase the search traffic on that page but can also result in users assuming that everything can be searched from that target (Lown, Sierra, and Boyer 2013).

Incorporating the service into a tabbed search box with options to search other services and resources is a popular method frequently featured on library homepages. Figure 8.2 is an illustration of a multitabbed search box with Summon as the open tab up-front and tabs for the catalog, databases, journal A-Z, and a general library website search also available. The downside of these tabbed interfaces is potentially making the search box too busy and confusing for users. The tabs behind the main open one may not receive as much notice or be used as frequently (Teague-Rector and Glaphery 2008).

Other custom search box options can be explored to provide users with more specific search interfaces when desired. Grand Valley State University, an early Summon adopter, uses Summon with default limiting to present search options for "search articles" and "find books and media" on its homepage (Daniels, Robinson, and Wishnetsky 2013).

Widgets can also be used to put a search box to another service inside the WSD main search or retrieval display screens. This is frequently done with chat assist applications or LibGuides content. They can also provide access to other outside content, such as YouTube or Google Scholar. There may be limits on the locations where these boxes can be inserted if this option is available.

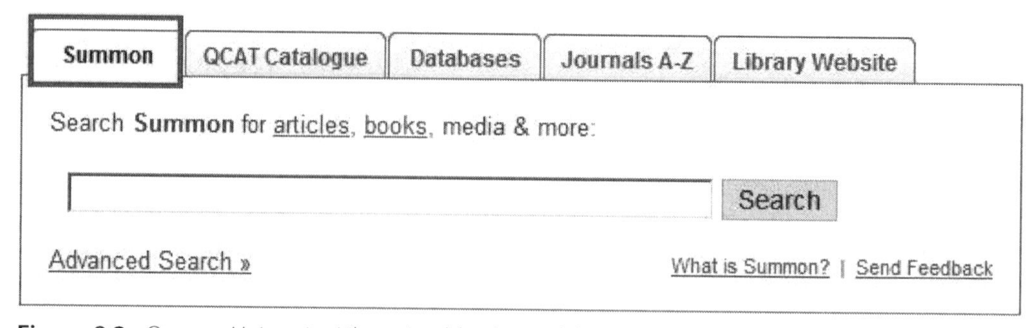

Figure 8.2. Queens University Library's tabbed search box with Summon. *Courtesy Queens University Libraries, Queens University, Kingston, Ontario.*

Customizing Facets and Filters

Facets and filters are essential to refining retrieval in WSD services. They allow a huge set of retrieval to be easily honed to a reasonable number by factors including content format, subject indexing, publication date, and source. Filters and facets typically appear in the left-hand column of the search results screen.

Filters are standard to most systems but can at times be tweaked or reordered to better match the needs of a library's user population. Typical filters include designating a publication date range, scope groups (e.g., "Full-Text Only," "Available in Library"), and broad content types (e.g., "Newspaper Content," "Academic Journals"). They generally appear above facet group options. Filters can be set to be automatically enabled by default. For example, a library could choose to enable the "Available in Library" limit to all searches to improve relevance and quality of retrieved content. This can be particularly important in academic or school environments where students are likely to look at and use just the first page of results. Asher et al. advocate setting filter defaults to maximize the value of resources that students encounter on that critical first page of search hits (Asher, Duke, and Wilson 2013).

Facets are derived from the metadata in the content sources included in the central index. The facets that appear depend on the metadata present, but some are so common that they will appear in almost all installations. Typical facet offerings appear in the textbox.

Less typical but frequently present facet groups include Geography, Library Location for multilibrary implementations, Genre, and Call Number range. Content sources with scientific research-based publications may also provide facets such as Age to help isolate particular research subjects or demographics, and content sources with business-focused resources may populate a Company Name facet.

Early on in the development of WSD systems, there were more facets that reflected more granularity in the metadata. As discussed in chapter 4, this was a mixed blessing,

TEXTBOX 8.2.

COMMON FILTER AND FACET OPTIONS AVAILABLE ON WEB-SCALE DISCOVERY SERVICES

Filters

- Content type (newspaper content, peer reviewed, academic journal)
- Full-text only
- Available in library

Facets

- Content provider
- Subject
- Publication
- Language
- Author

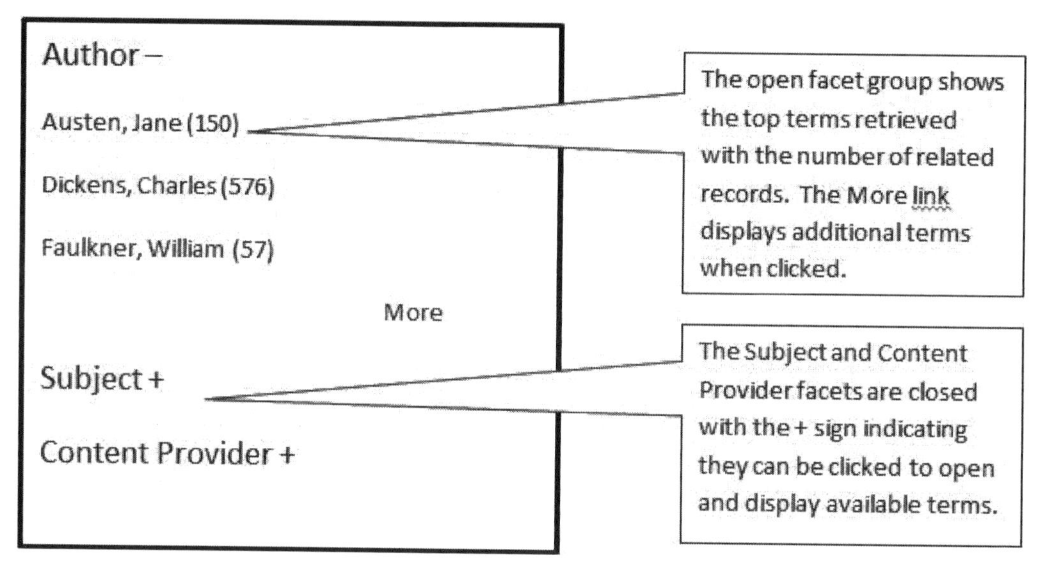

Figure 8.3. Open vs. closed facet groups.

as selecting a facet that reflected metadata in an individual content source frequently dropped relevant content from sources that lacked that particular index field. These days there seems to be a movement to simplify to the most common fields and consolidate. For example, EDS reduced three different subject facets to one unified subject facet group.

Subscribers can frequently choose which facets to include from a list of delivered facets derived from common index fields. The order of facets can often be changed, and the facet group can be configured to be open by default, displaying terms to select. Figure 8.3 is a mock-up of what facets from a system might look like, with the author facet open and the subject and content provider facets closed. Users can click on the closed facets to see the terms available to select. Subscribers can decide which facets make the most sense to display open, but keep in mind that having many facets open will push the following facets down the screen and out of the notice of users.

Libraries with specialized or local content that gets incorporated into the central index may have unique metadata to develop a facet group around. For example, a local genealogy database may have a field for birth date that could be a useful facet for searchers. In these cases, the library will need to work with the vendor to develop a custom facet. The metadata field will need to be indexed when records are brought into the central index to create a facet. The ease or difficulty of doing this will depend on the WSD product.

Sometimes libraries with a common subject specialty will find the need for facets unique to their content. If enough libraries are vocal about the need for a particular facet, the vendor will have incentive to develop it as a delivered facet.

Optimizing Retrieval Display

The brief and full record displays in WSD systems can often be customized to suit local needs. The search results page with brief records listed can typically be customized in the following ways:

- Page layout
- Number of records displayed on a page

- Default sort to use for display
- Record elements to display
- Material-type icons
- Incorporation of jacket art or other enhanced content

Page Layout

WSD systems run the gamut from having delivered page layouts that do not provide customization to being completely customizable. EDS, which falls somewhat between, allows libraries to have a two- or three-column layout for retrieval display. The three-column option provides a column for limits and facets to the left, search retrieval in the middle, and integrated resources and image previews to the right. In the two-column view, the right-hand column is closed but can be opened with a click. Primo allows several customization options, including "tiling," which componentizes elements of the results screens into separate tiles that can be reordered with the custom view editor (Bales and Dehmlow 2012). Most systems also allow extensive customization via API, including exporting search retrieval to other services or discovery layers.

Number of Records Displayed

Most systems default to displaying 10 to 25 records per page, but this can frequently be increased to 50 or more or sometimes decreased. The length of the brief record should be considered when opting for a default. Longer brief records may call for fewer records displayed per page.

This setting is often something that a user can change within account settings or a Preferences menu. If it is changed within account settings, it will be remembered for the next time that the user logs in.

Default Sort

The record sort for retrieval is set to relevancy ranked for WSD systems. Relevancy ranking is essential to bringing the best results to the top of the retrieval set. However, most systems allow for chronological sort options (most recent to oldest and vice versa). WorldCat Discovery Service also allows sorting by author and title. The system may allow the default for this setting to be changed from relevancy ranking, but libraries should consider the consequences of changing this very important tool. Sorting options frequently appear at the top of the results display as a drop-down menu or radio button for users to change on the fly when desired.

Record Elements to Display

While some systems allow for near-total control of which fields will be displayed in brief results (e.g., Primo), others have predefined record views with more or fewer fields that can be selected. Abstracts and/or index terms take up a lot of real estate but communicate up-front the potential value of a record. Libraries will need to weigh the importance of displaying this information versus having a cleaner display that shows more records. Summon includes a pop-up preview that displays all the record metadata, but users need to know to hover on the hyperlinked title to see it. EDS has options to include previews of images from retrieved publications in the brief record view.

The full record view page, when present, displays all the available metadata, including the abstract. Summon dispenses with the full record view, opting instead for the pop-up preview mentioned previously and direct link to the citation or full text within the content provider's interface. For catalog records, the location and status data for items held by the library display (in a consortium installation, it can include the holdings of multiple libraries). The labels used can be customized during catalog configuration, which takes place when the system is being implemented (see chapter 7). Both EDS and WorldCat Discovery Service have an option to present display of related editions and works (a FRBR-ized view) in the full record view, which can be turned on or off. WorldCat Discovery Service also presents holdings of the libraries that the subscriber designated as the second-tier-related collections. This group of libraries is determined by the subscriber during configuration.

Material-Type Icons

The search retrieval page usually includes material-type icons for each record to communicate the type of material represented in the search hits. For example, book records would be accompanied by a book image, while software and videodiscs are often associated with a CD-ROM image. The services all have a default set of buttons that can be used. However, subscribers can typically upload and use their own custom icons if they have preferred images. Libraries can also control what material types are associated with which icon for catalog and local content as part of the initial load configuration process. Many ILS systems include a bibliographic type or item-type field that can be associated with specific icons.

Incorporation of Jacket Art, Other Enriched Content, and Social Media

Jacket art images in brief and full record displays help to make a WSD service more graphically engaging for users. The services frequently allow for use of images from open-access sources such as Google Books and WorldCat. Amazon book jacket images can be used, but Amazon requires an active link to the Amazon record button when its art is used.

Many libraries subscribe to third-party content enrichment services to supply jacket art, table of contents, summaries, and reviews to the catalog and discovery services. Common services are Syndetics, Content Café, and LibraryThing for Libraries. All these elements can typically be incorporated and displayed in the full record view, and some elements, including jacket art, can appear in the brief record on the search retrieval page.

Primo and WorldCat Discovery Service both have native social networking features providing ratings, tagging, and reviews that can be turned on or off. EBSCO works closely with Chilifresh to incorporate this content for EDS subscribers when desired. These features are usually included in the full record view display. WorldCat Discovery Service can also include editorial reviews from We Read and GoodReads for subscribing libraries.

Creating Specialized Profiles

Often, for the price of one system, the subscriber can get several. WSD systems frequently allow for multiple implementations or separate profiles on a system. This accommodates consortium subscribers and academic campuses, school systems, or public library systems with multiple libraries. Each library can have its unique implementation. Even single library subscribers can benefit by setting up profiles to serve a specific audience. Profiles can be distinguished in the following ways:

Unique branding—Each library can incorporate its own logos or links.

Default limits to scope retrieval—Defaults can be set to limit automatically to location, language, content type, and so on.

Selective content—Content sources can be selected for inclusion or exclusion from the central index to deliver subject-specific content. Summon has delivered discipline scopes to aid in selecting for content in this way.

Each profile has a unique base URL/domain that can be used for search widgets or can be embedded in websites for multilibrary and consortium settings. There can sometimes be challenges with providing site-specific scoping to reflect individual licenses and subscriptions to content. See chapter 5, which discusses consortium and multilibrary implementation in further depth.

Single library sites can provide a search box associated with a specialized profile to embed in webpages or services for users desiring a custom interface. For example, a profile tailored to business sources could be embedded in a public library's webpage for business research and information.

Having multiple instances or profiles increases the workload in terms of both initial system configuration and ongoing maintenance. Libraries will need to weigh the increased effort with the benefit of providing these specialized portals. Sometimes a search widget will provide the option of default limiting to target-specific resources or formats without the need to set up and administer a separate profile.

TEXTBOX 8.3.

COMMON SEARCH INTERFACE CONFIGURATION AND CUSTOMIZATION TASKS

Branding

1. Develop or identify existing logo images to incorporate into the site.
2. Determine if custom CSS to match the appearance of the library's web presence is desired and within the scope of library staff members to provide and maintain it.

Tailoring Menu Bars, Links, and Labels

1. Establish where custom linking out from the service can be incorporated on search and retrieval pages.
2. Determine what services or search aids should be incorporated beyond a link to the library's homepage and search help (chat box if available).

(continued)

TEXTBOX 8.3. *Continued*

3. Provide a way for users to easily establish a new search that does not include limits applied to the previous search.
4. Look at default labeling throughout the service, and identify those that should be changed to eliminate confusion for searchers.

Constructing Search Boxes and Widgets

1. Establish how the search box will be incorporated into the library's homepage.
2. Determine if a simple keyword search box or one with more advanced search features will be presented, and use search widget construction tools or the administrative portal to develop the HTML.
3. Identify other library webpages or services where a search box for the service should be imbedded.
4. Decide if search widgets from other services should be included in the search interface or retrieval pages.

Facet and Limit Customization

1. Determine if limits should be presented in a different order or if any should be enabled by default (i.e., default to no newspaper content or to full-text retrieval only).
2. Likewise, determine order for default facets and decide if any should be eliminated.
3. Decide which facets will be displayed as open (showing a list of the search terms to select) and which as closed (requiring a click to see selections).
4. Based on local content metadata, identify any potential custom facets that would benefit users. Explore with the vendor how this custom facet can be developed.

Configuring Retrieval Display

1. Investigate layout options and decide if customization is desirable and feasible with available local and vendor support.
2. Decide how many records to display on the initial search retrieval page and what record elements to include in the brief and full record display (if allowed).
3. Determine if relevancy-ranked display should not be the default. Ensure that other sort options are visible to users.
4. During catalog configuration, determine how local holdings location and status displays will be labeled. For multilibrary implementations, decide what holdings from other library collections should display.
5. Decide whether to turn on a FRBR-ized view (showing other editions or formats) for full record display if available.
6. Assign which material types to associate with which material-type icon images, and determine which field in the local record will be used to identify material type.

7. Decide if custom material-type icons should be used, and inquire with the vendor how these can be incorporated.

Jacket Art, Other Enriched Content, and Social Media

1. Decide which open-access jacket art source will be incorporated, or identify a third-party provider for this content.
2. Determine what other enriched content to provide in full record view if using an enriched content vendor such as Syndetics or LibraryThing for Libraries.
3. Decide which social media features (e.g., ratings, tagging, and reviews) to turn on for users if provided by the vendor.

Creating Specialized Profiles

1. If in a multilibrary system, determine if separate profiles will provide the level of local customization desired by each individual library.
2. Identify services or webpages where a specially scoped instance of the service could be beneficial.
3. Determine if a separate profile is required or if a prescoped search widget can be developed to achieve the same benefit.

Key Points

All WSD services provide means to customize the appearance and functionality of the search interface. Libraries can opt for basic branding to incorporate a unique service name and logo, or they can incorporate cascading style sheets (CSS) to provide as close a match to the library's web presence as possible. Search widgets featuring the WSD service can be developed for placement on the library's homepage or wherever the option to search the service could be beneficial. This allows imbedding the search in places where users already are, including course management systems or departmental webpages.

Subscribers can also customize or develop facet options in the service to optimize searching on the local metadata available. Limits can be predefined to tailor search retrieval. Search retrieval pages can be configured to incorporate search widgets from other services and provide more or less metadata up-front in brief record displays. Content enrichment services can be incorporated to provide jacket art, table of contents, summaries, and reviews in full record view. Libraries will frequently have the option to include social media services through either the native interface or third-party vendors.

WSD services also will provide options for developing separate profiles that can be tailored to the needs of a particular audience, library, or service. Libraries will need to weigh the benefits of developing separate profiles with the time and labor required to configure and maintain them.

References

Asher, Andrew D., Linda M. Duke, and Suzanne Wilson. 2013. "Paths of Discovery: Comparing the Search Effectiveness of EBSCO Discovery Service, Summon, Google Scholar, and Conventional Library Resources." *College and Research Libraries* 74, no. 5: 464–88.

Bales, Aaron B., and Mark Dehmlow. 2012. "Implementing Primo for the Michiana Academic Library Consortium (MALC)." In *Planning and Implementing Resource Discovery Tools in Academic Libraries*, edited by Mary Pagliero Popp and Diane Dallis, 562–79. Hershey, PA: IGI Global.

Daniels, Jeffrey, Laura Robinson, and Susan Wishnetsky. 2013. "Results of Web-Scale Discovery: Data, Discussions, and Decisions." *Serials Librarian* 64, no. 1: 81–87.

Foster, Anita K., and Sarah C. Williams. 2012. "Early Adoption: EBSCO Discovery Service at Illinois State University." In *Planning and Implementing Resource Discovery Tools in Academic Libraries*, edited by Mary Pagliero Popp and Diane Dallis, 488–98. Hershey, PA: IGI Global.

Lown, Cory, Tito Sierra, and Josh Boyer. 2013. "How Users Search the Library from a Single Search Box." *College and Research Libraries* 74, no. 3: 227–41. http://crl.acrl.org/content/74/3/227.full.pdf.

Luther, Judy, and Maureen C. Kelly. 2011. "The Next Generation of Discovery." *Library Journal* 136, no. 5: 66–71. http://www.libraryjournal.com/lj/home/889250-264/the_next_generation_of_discovery.html.csp.

Teague-Rector, Susan, and James Ghaphery. 2008. "Designing Search: Effective Search Interfaces for Academic Library Web Sites." *Journal of Web Librarianship* 2, no. 4: 479–92.

CHAPTER 9

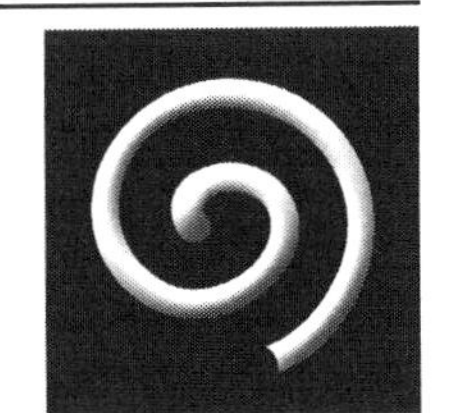

Introducing the Service to Users

IN THIS CHAPTER

- ▷ Releasing the Service to Library Users
- ▷ Marketing the Service
- ▷ Educating Staff and Users

Releasing the Service to Library Users

THE TIME REQUIRED TO IMPLEMENT a WSD service and get it ready for release is highly variable, depending on the degree of customization desired and whether the purchaser plans a soft launch of the service or not. Most libraries will want to launch the service as quickly as reasonable. Evaluation and selection is typically a several-month-long process, and once a contract is signed, the clock starts to tick on the subscription year.

A soft launch quickly puts a system into production, in a beta status. The service is clearly labeled as being in beta, or a trial status, and users are encouraged to provide feedback as they use it. A survey or feedback form is frequently integrated into the service's interface, or a link is provided somewhere within the search box. This allows the library to get the service into user's hands promptly while providing the freedom to continue refining the interface. The risk is that a system that has too many issues out of the box can be a turnoff to both users and library staff.

A launch with a prior implementation and test phase out of the public eye may be preferred if the library can afford to pay for a system that is not in actual production for a few weeks or possibly months. This will be necessary for systems that are highly tailored to the local environment. Releasing internally to staff first provides time to test the service with "real world" searches and get reference and instructional staff comfortable with it. Structured usability testing prior to release will also provide a way to identify the most egregious problems and pitfalls and get them resolved before wide exposure to users. Usability testing is discussed in detail in chapter 10.

Timing of the release may need to be in tandem with the end of a service contract for another discovery or federated search service. If so, make sure that an adequate window is allowed for completion of implementation tasks and testing. The library's webpage may also require significant redesign to allow for placement of a prominent search box or other access point to the service. In an academic or school environment, release of the service may be scheduled to occur at the beginning of a school year or semester to allow for introduction of the service in orientations or training sessions.

Marketing the Service

Even though a WSD service is frequently featured prominently with a search box front and center in a library's web presence, marketing is still required to make sure that library users understand what the search box is and what it is searching. Marketing encompasses both brand development and promotion via traditional means and social networking. It can also be done in tandem with training and instruction for the new service.

As with all marketing, the message is primary. Determine what two or three things users need to know about the service, and deliver that message consistently. For example, the message could be

- an easy Google-like search experience,
- convenient access to full-text resources,
- a comprehensive search entry point to the library's resources,

or some variation, depending on what the library wants to emphasize about the needs that this service will fulfill at the institution.

Of vital importance is acceptance and enthusiasm for the service among library staff members. Librarians who are not convinced of the value of the service or its place in the variety of search services being offered by the library will not be enthusiastic about promoting or teaching it. Reference, instruction, and outreach staff frequently control the message in both formal and informal instruction and search assistance. They can be of tremendous help in getting the word about a new service out.

An effective, catchy local name for the WSD system can also greatly help increase awareness of the service among library users. More important, because web-scale discovery services are frequently a novelty, a good name can play an important role in communicating what the service is. Because so much hinges on a good name for the service, selecting it should be something that is carefully considered. Many WSD service names include the one-search concept. Some libraries target the content more directly by using the concept of "articles plus books." Emphasis on the single search box is also frequently utilized. To further personalize a system, the library or institution name can be incorporated. At a college, university, or school, the mascot or school nickname could be used. Corporations, public library systems, and consortia can take the same approach with a unique name, acronym, community name, or a product cleverly tied in.

TEXTBOX 9.1.

NAMES FOR WEB-SCALE DISCOVERY SERVICES

ArticlesPlus

BOSS (Big Orange Search System at Oklahoma State University)

CatSearch (Montana State University Bobcats)

Findit

OneSearch@IU (Indiana University Libraries)

scoUT (University of Texas)

SearchBox

WCC Single Search (Wayne County Community College)

Successful names are concise, easy to say and remember, are frequently tailored to the institution, and help communicate what the system is. The textbox has some names currently in use at libraries with web-scale discovery services.

At Northumbria University, which implemented Summon in 2010, the established name of NORA (Northumbria Online Research Access) was retained but enhanced with "Power Search." This allowed it to be marketed as an upgrade to the existing discovery service. Posters and flyers were developed with the NORA Power Search branding (Thoburn, Coates, and Stone 2012).

Tie-in of a graphically interesting logo will help attract attention to the WSD service wherever it is placed on the library website or in other services. American University's SearchBox service incorporates a compass/lodestar image as the "o" in Box, creating a clever and meaningful logo. Montana State University incorporated a cat's-eye logo for the CatSearch branding derived from the school's Bobcat mascot (figure 9.1). Oklahoma State uses the color orange prominently in promoting BOSS (Big Orange Search Service). All these ideas can be incorporated into traditional print or online marketing campaigns.

Marketing can be combined with user education by sponsoring and promoting training sessions, brown-bag lunch sessions, or other informal instruction for the service in tandem with release. If the service is launched at the beginning of a semester in a school or university environment, promotion and instruction during orientation sessions provide an introduction to the service for incoming students.

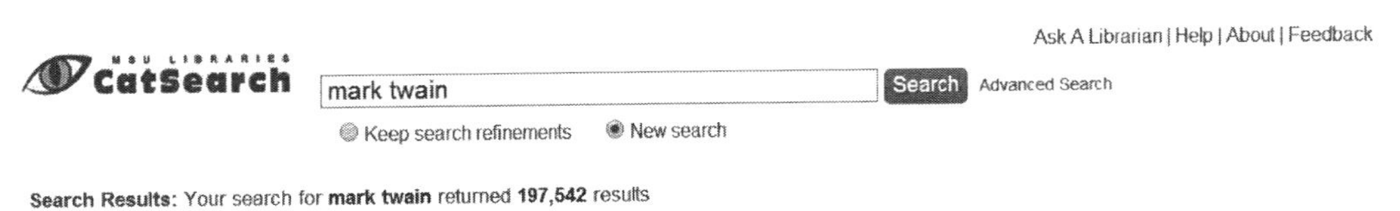

Figure 9.1. Montana State University's CatSearch branding. *Courtesy Montana State University Library, Montana State University, Bozeman, MT.*

TEXTBOX 9.2.

IMPLEMENTING WEB-SCALE DISCOVERY IN A SECONDARY SCHOOL: AN INTERVIEW WITH TIA ESPOSITO, LIBRARIAN, BOSTON COLLEGE HIGH SCHOOL

Who uses the library, and who did you hope to serve with a web-scale discovery service?

We are a middle/high school library serving approximately 1,800 students in grades 7–12. We hoped to serve this population better with a web-scale discovery service which we present to our students as the "Google" of all of our library online resources.

What were the key features you were looking for in a web-scale discovery product?

The most important feature we were looking for as a high school was for a search product that would be competitive with Google. Students want a one-stop shopping experience when it comes to online library services. They would like for a Google search to meet all of their information needs, but this is not possible, especially at the advanced levels and higher grades.

What was the biggest challenge/difficulty in implementation?

The biggest hurdle we felt was the negativity or nay-saying from fellow librarians at other private and independent schools with whom we are in collaboratives/consortium groups (it made us wonder if this were really the next step we should be taking toward our next-gen library services). However, it is reassuring to see that several are now jumping on the bandwagon and subscribing to web-scale discovery services themselves.

What kind of education or training did you offer to staff and students?

The librarians had orientations for all faculty, staff, and students at the start of the school year (as it was not fully implemented until the end of our school year last year).

Have you done anything to determine success of the service/user satisfaction (usability testing, surveys, other)?

Typically, we would implement such evaluation methods to determine user satisfaction; however, as the product has pretty much sold itself and has been such an overwhelming success (students actually applauding after orientation classes to finally see a product that for them rivals Google but with better library resources), we haven't as of yet conducted such an evaluation as it has not been implemented for a full year as of yet.

What advice would you have for other secondary school libraries considering a web-scale discovery service?

I would highly recommend a web-scale discovery service to all high schools both public and private for several reasons. First, students today have grown up in the information age (they are digital natives), and they have the expectation of being able to find everything they need for research and leisure online. Second, not only do they have this expectation, but they also have been raised on "Google"—the single "magical" search box—that they *want* to be able to use for all their information needs; however, this is not a reality (not yet anyway) when it comes to research for their school projects. As a school librarian, I feel a certain imperative to make sure that my students are college ready. When they go on to college, I want them to be "information literate" and feel comfortable with their future, more advanced research projects. A web-scale discovery service—again, as we have introduced it to the students as "the Google of our library resources"—exposes our students to scholarly, academic, peer-reviewed materials, which in turn they subsequently use for their projects or personal research and, moving forward, have a familiarity with the different kinds of information that are available from a basic Google search as opposed to more in-depth scholarly research.

Educating Staff and Users

Before the service goes into general release, library staff must be prepared to use and support it. The need for staff orientation and education should not be underestimated, especially in environments where staff members are less technologically nimble or comfortable with adopting new search interfaces. Michiana Academic Library Consortium, which implemented Primo, found that both staff and users with "a more traditional orientation to library research" needed extra help with the transition. They spent significant time on training and Q&A sessions for staff to build their skills with the interface (Bales and Dehmlow 2012).

> These sessions have bought quite a bit of good will, empowered staff to build expertise with the system, and even uncovered some complex techniques for searching Primo for library staff who may want advanced capabilities for finding research materials. (575)

Beyond just being familiar with the search interface, reference and instructional staff should have a good understanding of what web-scale discovery services are and how they function. Being familiar with the inner workings of the service and local configuration decisions will provide the expertise required to assist users and help troubleshoot issues as they arise.

The ease of the search interface may lead some libraries to decide not to do a focused instructional outreach. This decision is largely dependent on the user population. To date, most WSD services have been implemented in academic library environments. Some of these libraries have reported extensive instructional campaigns, as at Bowling Green State University, which implemented Summon in 2010. They taught Summon to students, faculty, and staff in one-shot class sessions, workshops, and learning communities and during individual interactions (Cardwell, Lux, and Snyder 2012).

At Grand Valley State, also an early Summon adopter, classroom librarians opted to teach Summon since it was felt to be more effective to teach in the hour of instruction allowed for incoming freshman than trying to teach the intricacies of the myriad other database platforms. Showing advanced search features in Summon gave students strategies

TEXTBOX 9.3.

WHAT TO INCLUDE IN USER INSTRUCTION

- Explain what is included in the web-scale discovery service and what is not; make users aware of subject-specific alternatives.
- Discuss relevancy ranking and how it works; show why sources were retrieved for a particular search.
- Demonstrate how to narrow search retrieval with filters and facets; if some filters are on by default, explain why, and show how the filter can be removed.
- Show users the Advanced Search screen and strategies for successful known item searching.
- For undergraduate and secondary school students, discuss different formats and how to distinguish and limit to them.
- Explain why some content types are more authoritative, and show how to limit to peer-reviewed and scholarly sources.
- For more advanced audiences, demonstrate phrase searching, proximity operators, wildcards, and how to search on stop words.
- Demonstrate user account functions and search retrieval management tools; show academic students citation generation features.
- Show how to report problems with the service and how to get to help via chat, FAQs, or tutorials.

that could be applied to other database interfaces. Demonstrating features such as saving searches and e-mailing results was thought to "help . . . win trust in the library as the best place to start their research" (Daniels, Robinson, and Wishnetsky 2013, 83).

Several libraries have reported that a major challenge for undergraduate students using WSD services is not with the actual search interface but with evaluating retrieval. Cardwell, Lux, and Snyder (2012) reported that first- and second-year undergraduate students were comfortable with searching the interface but had trouble with the lack of context for the multiple formats being retrieved. They determined that students could benefit from instruction about the different publication types being retrieved. Similarly, Gross and Sheridan (2011) reported that undergraduates found useful information quickly but had little concept of the format of the materials retrieved. The researchers questioned whether the students fully understood what they were finding.

> Thus the simplicity of the new interface may be doubled edged. On the one hand it gives students confidence. Yet, on the other hand, this does not mean they have any great understanding of information seeking or evaluation of resources. . . . It would seem that, as librarians, our role in helping students understand how to use the interface to find data may be diminishing; but conversely, our role in helping them to develop search strategies and evaluate what is useful information becomes even more important. (245)

With the introduction of these services, the role of the library in instruction may need to shift away from focusing on teaching the actual search interface to distinguishing differences in format, the source of the data found, and the relative quality and value of that information.

Having instructional tools that can be accessed when users are searching from home or dorm rooms is important, particularly in environments where there is emphasis on online courses or remote services. At Montana State University, usage statistics indicated that users turned to online help as they searched Summon. This emphasized the need for easy access to chat, e-mail, and telephone reference assistance from within the search interface. Librarians also developed guides and tutorials at the point of need (Babbitt, Foster, and Rossmann 2012). Many libraries provide search FAQs and help pages that can be linked to from within the service with information on advanced searching features, such as phrase searching, proximity indicators, wildcards, and stop words.

TEXTBOX 9.4.

COMMON TASKS WHEN RELEASING WEB-SCALE DISCOVERY SERVICES TO USERS

Releasing the Service

1. Decide whether to do a soft launch that puts the service into immediate release in a beta status or to have a period where the service is configured and customized in-house and beta tested by staff.
2. For beta release, build means of communicating feedback from users into the service.
3. Identify a time for release that coincides with opportunities for promotion and training, as in start of school year in academic and school settings.

Marketing the Service

1. Determine what two to three things users need to know about the new service, and feature this message in print and social media–focused marketing.
2. Make sure reference and instructional staff are knowledgeable and enthusiastic about the service and prepared to promote it in formal and informal instructional situations.
3. Establish a name for the service that is concise and communicates what it is to users.
4. Build visually engaging branding for the service that features the name.

Educating Staff and Users

1. Give staff adequate time to learn to use the service in advance of release to users. Some staff may require extra help to make the adjustment.
2. Decide if a focused instructional outreach is required for users, and prepare a strategy for teaching it in formal and informal venues.
3. Adjust instruction to focus less on how to search the interface and more on distinguishing material types, sources of data, and quality of sources retrieved.
4. Develop remote and online instruction and assistance methods, including FAQs, online tutorials, and easy access to reference chat services.

Key Points

Because a subscription year begins when a service is purchased, libraries will need to decide whether to put a system immediately into service in a beta status or allow time for customization, possible usability testing, and further adjustments from out-of-the-box settings. Release may be scheduled to coincide with the beginning of a school year or another time when it can be promoted and taught in tandem with orientations.

Marketing includes naming the service, developing branding, and marketing a message that is promoted through print and social media and can be combined with instruction. Education and instructional efforts should start with staff to ensure that they are comfortable with the service and have the skills to teach and troubleshoot issues. User instruction will depend on the audience and may vary from a multipronged educational campaign to providing minimal instruction in orientations and at point of need. Libraries that have a large remote user group should make sure that online tutorials and integrated chat assistance are available.

References

Babbit, Elizabeth P., Amy Foster, and Doralyn Rossmann. 2012. "Implementation of Resource Discovery: Lessons Learned." In *Planning and Implementing Resource Discovery Tools in Academic Libraries*, edited by Mary Pagliero Popp and Diane Dallis, 580–97. Hershey, PA: IGI Global.

Bales, Aaron B., and Mark Dehmlow. 2012. "Implementing Primo for the Michiana Academic Library Consortium (MALC)." In *Planning and Implementing Resource Discovery Tools in Academic Libraries*, edited by Mary Pagliero Popp and Diane Dallis, 562–79. Hershey, PA: IGI Global.

Cardwell, Catherine, Vera Lux, and Robert J. Snyder. 2012. "Beyond Simple Easy and Fast: Reflections on Teaching Summon." *College and Research Libraries News* 73, no. 6: 344–47.

Daniels, Jeffrey, Laura Robinson, and Susan Wishnetsky. 2013. "Results of Web-Scale Discovery: Data, Discussions, and Decisions." *Serials Librarian* 64, no. 1: 81–87.

Gross, Julia, and Lutie Sheridan. 2011. "Web Scale Discovery: The User Experience." *New Library World* 112, nos. 5/6: 236–47.

Thoburn, Jane, Annette Coates, and Graham Stone. 2012. "Simplifying Resource Discovery and Access in Academic Libraries: Implementing and Evaluating Summon at Huddersfield and Northumbria Universities." In *Planning and Implementing Resource Discovery Tools in Academic Libraries*, edited by Mary Pagliero Popp and Diane Dallis, 598–607. Hershey, PA: IGI Global.

CHAPTER 10

Usability Testing of Web-Scale Discovery Services

IN THIS CHAPTER

Conducting Usability Tests

Why Do Usability Testing?

USABILITY TESTING PROVIDES LIBRARIES THE OPPORTUNITY to make a controlled and unbiased evaluation of the effectiveness of a searching tool or website. There is a rich history of usability testing for library websites and an emerging body of research on usability testing of discovery tools. Prior to the emergence of web-scale discovery services, next-generation catalogs and federated search tools were evaluated in this way with a number of studies published. Denton and Coysh provide a summary of the history of usability testing on next-gen catalog discovery interfaces up through the time of their study of VuFind in 2011.

More recently, a number of usability studies on WSD services have been published, with all the services having been studied in various academic environments. It is still hard to draw broad conclusions based on the variations in local configurations and differences in study design, as observed by Jody Condit Fagan et al. (2012) in their usability study of EDS. They cite the need for additional usability studies to improve the content, design, and user interfaces of available services and to inform local institutional decisions regarding configuration and customization.

As mentioned previously, the majority of usability testing on discovery services and WSD services in particular has been done in academic environments. There is a need to learn more about how users in public library, school library, and special library environments use the services and if their searching needs are being met.

Usability tests can be done in conjunction with trials of WSD systems under consideration to help identify the best candidates for purchase. Keep in mind that this testing will be most effective if a custom trial incorporating local data has been supplied. Usability testing can also be done postpurchase and after initial configuration to identify potential issues with the local implementation prior to general release to users.

Usability Test Methods

There are several excellent publications on usability testing of library websites, including Norlin and Winter's *Usability Testing for Library Websites: A Hands-On Guide*, published in 2002. Although written specifically for website testing, the principles apply well to testing discovery services. Rubin and Chisnell's *Handbook of Usability Testing: How to Plan, Design, and Conduct Effective Tests*, published in 2008, is also recommended. This section briefly addresses the overall structure of most usability tests and tasks associated. Libraries considering usability testing should consult the more in-depth publications and study previously published usability tests of WSD systems.

- Study recruitment
- Prestudy survey
- Study administration and observation methods
- Tasks/questions
- Poststudy survey

Study Recruitment

Doing a usability test does not require a large-scale recruitment effort. As demonstrated in a frequently referenced paper by Nielsen (2000), only five participants will reveal 75% of the issues with an interface in a well-designed study. Libraries doing usability testing will typically try to secure at least one representative from each constituent group that will be using the system. In academic libraries, that means representatives from undergraduate student, graduate student, and faculty populations. In a public library environment, it might mean recruiting a variety of age levels and users with varying degrees of comfort with search systems. Depending on the scope of the study, certain populations might be targeted for nonparticipation. In Majors's (2012) study of four discovery products, novice searchers were desired, and potential participants who had worked for the library in the past were not eligible.

In some environments—particularly, hospital, health care, and academic institutions that conduct research on human subjects—an institutional review board (IRB) may need to approve the study before recruitment can commence. IRBs exist to ensure that studies involving human subjects are conducted ethically and that subjects are not harmed or taken advantage of in any way. In these cases, the study protocol and recruitment methods will need to be submitted to the board. A consent form may also need to be developed and given to participants in advance of their participating in the study. Majors includes the consent form used in his study as an appendix to his article (202). Check in advance to see if IRB approval is required before starting recruitment.

Libraries seeking study participants can put the word out via social media, school or company Listservs, and e-mail distribution groups or through direct appeal at meetings or instructional sessions. Prospective study participants should be informed in advance of the time commitment and the need to be punctual and show up for the appointment.

Some libraries provide a small reward to participants to encourage participation. It should be enough of a reward to make the participants feel that their time and opinions are valued but not so generous that it encourages participants who are more interested in the gift than helping the library. A $5 gift card for the local coffee shop or credit toward printing or copying at the library is good potential incentive.

Prestudy Survey

Many usability studies will begin with a presurvey to establish some baseline information about the study participant. It may be useful to know if the participant used the system previously, one's opinion of other services that the library may be looking at replacing with a WSD service, or further demographic information about the participant that may be required for accurate results analysis. In the James Madison University study, participants were asked about their academic discipline and experiences with the library website, catalog, and the EBSCO*host* search interface, which is similar to the EDS system being tested (Fagan et al. 2012). Questions could also assess the pretest knowledge and opinion of the WSD service.

Study Administration and Observation Methods

There is usually at least one administrator of a usability test to guide the participant through the process. The need for the presence of an additional administrator is dependent on the availability of automated means of recording participant actions. In situations where there will be no automated methods used, one other staff member who is devoted to taking detailed notes will be required. Even if automated methods are used, it is still recommended to have a human note taker in case recordings fail or files are lost.

Software that records screen activity and user comments, such as Camtasia, can be used to capture each session. There is also software available for purchase that has been designed specifically for recording and conducting usability tests, including TechSmith's Morae and Usability Testing Environment. Both provide means of conducting unmediated tests. Though this may be appealing, human observation is frequently invaluable, and key insights may be missed by having the entire process done in an unmediated environment. If recordings are made, hours must be spent viewing and analyzing them.

At the beginning of each test session, the test administrator should introduce himself or herself and then read a script that explains the reason for the study and how it will be conducted. A script ensures that each test taker hears the same information. The script should include a warning that test administrators are simply observers and that they will not assist the participants in completing the tasks or in any way influence their actions. The script should also assure the participants that the system is what is being tested and not them; participants should not feel as if they failed if they struggle to finish a task. Above all, participants should be encouraged to vocalize their thought processes and express any satisfaction or dissatisfaction with the service as they work to complete the tasks.

TEXTBOX 10.1.

USABILITY TESTING SOFTWARE

For libraries that plan to do frequent usability testing on search interfaces and webpage design, usability testing software may be worth the investment. Academic libraries can inquire if the institution has purchased one of these systems and has it available for studies.

TechSmith's Morae: From the makers of Camtasia, Morae is a comprehensive usability testing product. It can also be used to record focus groups. It provides preset study templates, records data (including the user's facial and verbal interaction), and does results analysis. Free trials are available. http://www.techsmith.com/morae-features.html.

Bailey's Usability Testing Environment: UTE can be used in combination with Morae or on its own. It provides usability test creation tools, data capture, and report generation. When in combination with Morae, it will pinpoint key findings and insert marks in Morae recordings, making them easier to analyze. https://www.mindd.com/Content.aspx?pid=UTEStandard.

TechSmith's Camtasia: Though Camtasia was not designed specifically for usability testing, many libraries have it and use it to capture screen activity and audio of study participants. Camtasia is also frequently used to record tutorials. http://www.techsmith.com/camtasia.html.

Tasks/Questions

Because usability testing is being done to see how well the search interface meets users' searching and research needs, questions asked during the testing should reflect typical searches done by the user population. Tests of WSD systems have included the following types of tasks and questions:

- Find a (video, book, journal) on *X* subject.
- Find *X* book. Is it available for checkout?
- Find two peer-reviewed journal articles from the last five years on *X* topic.
- Find the journal *X*.
- Download the full text of an article on *X*.
- Find an article on *x* topic and e-mail it to a colleague.
- The library does not have *X* book. Request it via interlibrary loan.
- Find a way to ask a librarian for help with this search tool.

Sometimes tasks that are best accomplished by other services are included to see if users will try to do them within the WSD service or will utilize the links to other library services included in the interface. In the James Madison University study, users were asked to do the same task using the WSD service and not using it, to see which was more efficient (Fagan et al. 2012).

Usability tests should not include an overwhelming number of tasks. Ten should be considered the maximum. Methods may be developed to keep users from becoming bogged down or overwhelmed by an individual task. The James Madison University study set time limits for each question, which were enforced by the software used to conduct and record the study (Fagan et al. 2012). This could also be done by administrators of a study.

A method for scoring performance should be built into the tool used for data collection—for example, number of clicks required to complete a task, the amount of time taken, or the user's level of satisfaction with ease of completion. Completing a task to satisfaction can be left to users to decide or evaluated by test administrators.

Poststudy Survey

When the test is complete, a second survey is typically included to gather further data on the test taker's opinion of the system. Again, this survey should not include an overwhelming number of questions given the amount of time that the volunteer has already spent on completing the presurvey and the test tasks. The following are some typical questions included in postsurvey:

- Would you use this search tool if it was available?
- When would you use this search tool?
- What would you change about the search tool?
- What is easy to use about this search tool?
- What is difficult about this search tool?

An open-ended question is recommended regarding overall impressions of the system or inviting feedback on any area of concern or issue not included in the other postsurvey questions. The posttest survey should have a scoring method, such as a Likert scale, for results analysis.

Analyzing Results to Improve the Service

Once testing is completed, administrators will review and tabulate results. Some areas of weakness may become obvious to administrators as testing is taking place. Others may be revealed only as results are tabulated. Both the form for recording results of the tests and the postsurvey will need to have an evaluative method built in with baseline success/acceptability standards to assess which tasks are not meeting performance expectations. If the study is being published, statistical analyses should be applied to ensure that results are statistically relevant to support any conclusions reached.

In situations where usability testing is being done prior to purchase, tasks that do not meet performance standards should be discussed with the vendor. There may be adjustments that could be made or customizations that will improve performance. For example, if undesired types of materials are too frequently coming to the top of results, explore if relevancy ranking could be refined or if filters could be applied by default. It is hard to assess how much the system will improve in such situations unless the vendor is willing to apply them to the trial instance. If usability testing reveals serious issues with the interface, it is an indication that the system may not be a good match for the library.

When testing is done to assess a purchased system, tasks that do not meet performance standards point to areas that now require intervention and improvement. Some required changes may be readily apparent. During usability testing of EDS at Himmelfarb Health Sciences Library at George Washington University, users had difficulty recognizing the button for full-text via the link resolver. The button was revised to be larger and text on it more legible (Thompson, Obrig, and Abate 2013). When the issue is not so obviously or easily solved, discussion is advised with the vendor to explore what adjustments or customizations are possible. Talking with other customers in similar environments may also reveal strategies for addressing the identified issues. After changes have been applied, follow-up testing focused on just the problem areas can assess if the issues have been resolved. If not, explore possible enhancements with the vendor or user community. James Madison University suggested that EBSCO add material types for video and audio as a result of its usability test on EDS, and the vendor provided the change (Fagan et al. 2012).

TEXTBOX 10.2.

USABILITY TESTING TASKS

1. Read up on usability testing techniques and previous studies done on WSD services.
2. Recruit at least five individuals to participate who represent each of the core user groups that will be using the service.
3. Find out if it will be necessary to have Institutional Review Board approval. If required, submit study plans to the board well in advance, and develop a consent form.
4. Develop a prestudy survey for participants to discover more about their status and knowledge of the WSD service and other library services.
5. Identify two library staff members to serve as test administrators, directing test participants and recording notes about sessions.
6. Determine if automated recording methods or software to administer the study will be used.
7. Write a script that will be read to all test participants, explaining how the test will be administered and encouraging users to vocalize their thought processes.
8. Identify 10 or fewer tasks for test participants to complete, which replicate common searches that users will be doing on the service.
9. Define successful completion of a task, and develop a means for scoring performance.
10. Compose a poststudy survey to gather test participants' satisfaction with the service and invite other feedback. Develop a scoring method for the postsurvey.
11. Discuss tasks that did not meet performance standards with the vendor when usability testing is done as part of prepurchase evaluation, and explore if adjustments can be done to improve performance.
12. For purchased systems, make any obvious changes that can resolve issues revealed by testing. Explore with the vendor on issues that do not have an immediately apparent resolution and request system enhancements when necessary.

Examining Usability Studies of Web-Scale Discovery Services

Those embarking on usability studies can use previous studies as a model. Published studies that have been subjected to rigorous analysis can also provide insights into product strengths and weaknesses in certain situations and with particular populations. The following is a closer look at three recently published usability studies of web-scale discovery services.

Asher, Andrew D., Lynda M. Duke, and Suzanne Wilson. "Paths of Discovery: Comparing the Search Effectiveness of EBSCO Discovery Service, Summon, Google Scholar, and Conventional Library Resources." *College & Research Libraries* 74, no. 5 (2013): 464–88.

Participating libraries: Bertrand Library, Bucknell University; Ames Library, Illinois Wesleyan University.

Participant population: 87 undergraduate students.

Products tested: EDS, Summon, Google Scholar, native catalog interface/databases.

Tools used: Camtasia, Vovici web survey software, Nvivo data analysis software, SPSS statistics software.

Informed consent: IRB approval obtained and consent forms completed.

Participant gift: $10 and $20 credit to university bookstores.

Study Methods

Students from both institutions were randomly split into five groups to test each of the sources: EDS, Summon, Library Catalog/Databases, no tool specified (students had access to all resources). They were given four research questions similar to those that they might be given for a course assignment, and they were asked to find two resources that they would use to complete the assignment. This provided researchers information about how the participants approached searching and how they searched sources. In a second interview portion, they were asked open-ended questions about search practices and habits and how they evaluate resources.

Evaluation was based on time to complete tasks, number of page views, and total searches. Sources selected were also rated by a panel of four librarians, and the types of resources retrieved were totaled and compared.

Conclusions

Though, quantitatively, EDS was found to be the most effective and efficient of the four sources tested, authors caution users to look closer at the underlying causes of the results. Students in the Google Scholar and Summon groups both tended to pick lower-quality resources. The "no tool" group tended to pick webpages. Study authors attributed this to students' tendency to rely on relevancy-ranking effectiveness and only look at what is on the first page of search hits. Because Summon had more newspaper content, students in this group selected more newspaper resources. This emphasizes the importance of relevancy ranking and setting default filters to bring the best resources to the top of search results.

Fagan, Jody Condit, Meris A. Mandernach, Carl S. Nelson, Jonathan R. Paulo, and Grover Saunders. "Usability Test Results for a Discovery Tool in an Academic Library." *Information Technology and Libraries* 31, no. 1 (2012): 83–112.

Participating libraries: James Madison University Libraries.

Participant population: 10 students and 2 faculty members.

Products tested: EDS and the QuickSearch search widget.

Tools used: Morae and UTE.

Informed consent: IRB approval obtained and consent forms completed.

Participant gift: None mentioned.

Study Methods

Participants were given nine tasks reflective of typical patron requests, including finding articles on early childhood cognitive development, limiting retrieval by peer-reviewed sources and currency, finding the "Ask a Librarian" chat feature, and navigating from the discovery service to another database for a search. All tasks had set time limits, and some asked users to express their satisfaction with the answer found. Librarian observers also assessed success. At test conclusion, participants were presented with a 10-item System Usability Scale to rate the system on various aspects of usability. The study included pre- and posttest surveys to gather demographic information about participants, their knowledge of library search tools and resources, and their satisfaction with QuickSearch and EDS.

Conclusions

The study results led to some general observations of student usage of discovery tools and library resources and to some concrete changes in discovery tool configuration. Among the general findings, students have trouble distinguishing what can be searched in various systems (i.e., looking for articles in the library catalog.), and they are not good at identifying the best tool for a particular need. A few changes were made to EDS and QuickSearch as a result of study findings. Test participants had difficulty locating a specific journal title. A link for Journal A-Z was added to the QuickSearch widget. Test participants also did not use the federated search option in EDS, and low usage of this feature led James Madison University to abandon it and populate the right-side column with "Ask a Librarian," subject guides, and direct research database links.

Williams, Sarah C., and Anita K. Foster. "Promise Fulfilled? An EBSCO Discovery Service Usability Study." *Journal of Web Librarianship* 5, no. 3 (2011): 179–98.

Participating libraries: Milner Library, Illinois State University.

Participant population: 6 students (mostly upperclass and graduate).

Products tested: EDS and EBSCO*host* Integrated Search.

Tools used: Camtasia.

Informed consent: IRB approval obtained and consent forms completed.

Participant gift: $15 Amazon gift card and library T-shirt.

Study Methods

After three minutes of exploring Search It (EDS) on their own and stating what they thought it was and what it did, participants completed five research scenarios while observed by librarian mediators and recorded by Camtasia. Scenarios included finding a full-text article on bullying published since 2005 and opening it on the screen, as well as finding out if the library has a copy of "I Sing the Body Electric" in *Leaves of Grass.* The study included pre- and posttest questionnaires.

Conclusions

No study participants looked at results beyond the first page, and they were attracted to results with images (EDS includes images from retrieved records to display in search results.) Participants selected limiters more frequently at the beginning of the search, rather than applying them after retrieving an initial set of hits. Most frequently used postsearch limiters were toward the top of the page. Federated search sources (Integrated Search) were also underused, as in James Madison University's study. The overall takeaway was that students did not use many of the features available (facets, search management tools) and more needed to be done to make them apparent. Although students assessed Search It to be easy to use in the posttest survey, they agreed that instruction for the service would be helpful.

Key Points

Usability testing can be done as part of the evaluation period when considering a service for purchase or for a purchased service to identify areas where the system requires further configuration or changes. Five or more users reflecting the makeup of the user population for the service should be recruited. The study may require Institutional Review Board approval in educational or medical settings. Though studies can be designed to be unmediated if usability testing software is used, having staff administrators who can observe directly and act as backup should recording methods fail is recommended. Studies usually include a pretest survey, a series of tasks that are reflective of typical searches, and a posttest follow-up survey. An evaluative method should be built into the data collection instrument for the study to determine the tasks that were completed successfully and the level of user satisfaction. Discuss areas where the service fell short with the vendor to determine if adjustments can be made to improve performance. Consider requesting enhancements to the service for issues that cannot be easily resolved.

References

Denton, W., and S. J. Coysh. 2011. "Usability Testing of VuFind at an Academic Library." *Library Hi Tech* 29, no. 2: 301–19.

Fagan, Jody Condit, Meris A. Mandernach, Carl S. Nelson, Jonathan R. Paulo, and Grover Saunders. 2012. "Usability Test Results for a Discovery Tool in an Academic Library." *Information Technology and Libraries* 31, no. 1: 83–112.

Majors, Rice. 2012. "Comparative User Experiences of Next Generation Catalogue Interfaces." *Library Trends* 61, no. 1: 186–207.

Nielsen, Jakob. 2000. "Why You Only Need to Test with 5 Users." http://www.useit.com/alertbox/20000319.html.

Norlin, Elaina, and CM! Winters. 2002. *Usability Testing for Library Websites: A Hands-On Guide.* Chicago: American Library Association.

Rubin, Jeffrey, and Dana Chisnell. 2008. *Handbook of Usability Testing: How to Plan, Design, and Conduct Effective Tests.* Indianapolis, IN: Wiley.

Thompson, JoLinda, Kathe Obrig, and Laura Abate. 2013. "Web-Scale Discovery in an Academic Health Sciences Library: Development and Implementation of the EBSCO Discovery Service." *Medical Reference Services Quarterly* 32, no. 1: 26–41.

CHAPTER 11

Maintaining a Web-Scale Discovery Service

IN THIS CHAPTER

- ▷ Monitoring Systems Usage
- ▷ Administering Changes to the System and Troubleshooting Issues
- ▷ Managing Impacts to Collection Development, Document Delivery, and Cataloging
- ▷ Keeping Up with the Changing Market

Monitoring Systems Usage

USAGE DATA ON A WSD SERVICE CAN PROVIDE a window into how searchers are using it. Determining return on investment will be important for most libraries that invest in one of these systems, as not only the subscription fee but also the substantial time required to implement it need to be justified. Subscribing libraries will want to know if having the system improves the user's search experience and increases usage of the library's collections, particularly electronic full-text content.

All web-scale discovery systems provide a method for reporting out statistics. They range from basic counts of sessions, searches, and views of full text and abstracts to more sophisticated results, such as top-failed searches, breakdowns of searches by IP range, and usage of facet groups. More information about statistics available on the four WSD services is included in chapter 5.

Comparing the overall volume on the WSD service to searches on popular databases can help assess if it is supplanting other search tools and is valued by users. Be aware that sometimes a WSD service will report search volume against every content source queried, multiplying the number of searches by all the included content sources. This can greatly inflate the numbers. In these cases, the number of sessions may provide the more accurate number.

Number of full-text sources viewed/retrieved should be relatively high in relation to search sessions. If the number is falling well below a 1:1 ratio, it indicates that searches are not effective, full text is not available for desired sources, or there are issues with the link resolver that should be investigated. Another possibility is that the site is being exploited by searchers outside the institution's user population, who are unable to click through to full text for systems that allow guest access or otherwise do not require a log-in. Checking sessions by IP can help establish if this is the case.

Though the native statistics interface should provide good information on usage, there are other methods of tracking use and determining impact on collections usage. Libraries such as Grand Valley State have run statistical comparisons of their COUNTER statistics prior to implementation of a WSD service and after (Way 2010). This helped gauge the impact of the new service on resources at both the database/content source level and the individual title level. The link resolver being used in the WSD service will also be able to provide usage at the title level but may not supply where the original request was generated.

Monitoring usage at the database/content source or title level can provide a window into which resources are being used most heavily by searchers of the WSD service. An academic library that sees a jump in the number of news sources being utilized and a drop in the number of serious academic journals should investigate to make sure that users are not simply grabbing the top few items retrieved in systems where news sources are not blocked or suppressed by default.

Systems that report on search terms and strategies used provide important information on how users are searching. Several vendors report top searches with no hits, which can reveal either user misunderstanding of how the system works or weaknesses with the search interface that should be investigated further.

Google Analytics is another source of statistics that can be particularly useful for monitoring usage from embedded search boxes/widgets. Google Analytics tracks use statistics from particular webpages and locations, providing number of times that a site is visited, the amount of time spent there, and the user's home IP. If a library has multiple avenues for accessing the WSD service or multiple profiles established, Google Analytics could provide a way to monitor which of these are most used.

Administering Changes to the System and Troubleshooting Issues

As further discussed at the end of the chapter, WSD services are changing and evolving rapidly. New content sources are constantly being added, while some A&I databases or other sources may disappear from a system, depending on the state of the partnerships between publishers and the system vendor. Along with changes to content, the discovery layers are in a state of flux, as these systems become more refined and respond to demands from purchasers and users.

System administrators should be proactive to catch changes in the bud that have a potential negative impact. Regular monitoring of the search interface, system performance, and settings is good practice. Because WSD services interact with so many different systems (link resolvers, ILS systems, authentication services, networks, browsers, etc.), they will break in a variety of ways. After a year and a half of experience with an EDS implementation at University of Central Florida, Hoeppner (2013) reported numerous issues that required intervention:

- "Bad data" from content providers
- Various cookie, pop-up, and other browser issues
- "Myriad" article access problems
- Slow system response time

The library has a team of staff who work to troubleshoot issues as they arise, including cataloging, systems, and content specialists. She advises having problem report forms, replicating reported issues, and communicating clearly and in detail with the vendor to find a resolution.

Along with routine checking and troubleshooting, systems administrators and those closely involved with teaching users and providing support should subscribe to any Listservs, blogs, Twitter feeds, or newsletters available from the vendor for the user community. Major changes and enhancements to the services are frequently timed to coincide with events such as ALA midwinter and annual meetings. Monitoring meeting events and news, even if not attending, is recommended to keep abreast of changes. If attending, be sure to stop by the vendor booth in exhibits and look at what is being demonstrated.

Meeting with sales reps regularly and visiting the vendor's website is also a good way to stay informed. Many vendors offer regular webinar trainings and other outreach events to sell systems and keep current subscribers informed. Communication with the vendor should be a two-way street. Subscribers should share their experiences with the system and notify the vendor of any issues encountered or areas of weakness that cannot be easily resolved with troubleshooting or changes in configuration via the administrative portal. Developing relationships with other subscribers can be of value when lobbying for enhancements, changes in system behavior, or new sources of content.

System administrators should check with the vendor to be sure to get advance notifications of major software upgrades or changes in content. Any change or upgrade to software should be checked closely postinstallation to make sure local customizations, live item status information from the catalog, or other critical settings have not been broken or changed.

TEXTBOX 11.1.

PROACTIVE SYSTEM ADMINISTRATION TIPS

- Routinely perform test searches and test linking to full text.
- Maintain communications with reference and instructional staff, and regularly solicit direct feedback from users.
- Subscribe to vendor Listservs and Twitter feeds and monitor support websites.
- Communicate regularly with vendor sales and support reps.
- Closely monitor monthly systems statistics for usage trends.
- Check top searches with 0 or fewer than 50 results to see if adjustments in the search interface are required.
- Document all local configurations and customizations.

To be able to detect such changes and repair them, it is important to document all local settings. Any branding, local interface/appearance customizations, or API applications should have code and image files saved somewhere easily accessible. If there has been major customization of content sources, there should be a list of active sources that can be consulted after software upgrades or content changes to make sure that all the selected content is still feeding the service. Other settings, such as which facets are active and what the defaults are for record views, should likewise be documented somewhere where they can be easily referred to if necessary to restore. The original implementation questionnaire, with answers provided to the vendor, should also be saved somewhere for later referral if needed.

Managing Impacts to Collection Development, Document Delivery, and Cataloging

Collection Development

Having a web-scale discovery service in a library can have several important impacts on collection development activities. Most reports of impacts on collection usage post-WSD implementation reflect greater use of electronic full-text content to which the library subscribes. Some libraries reported declines in usage of some databases and physical collections (Kemp 2012; Way 2010).

West Carolina University purchased and implemented EDS in 2011. Due to uncertainty of funding after the second year, the library examined usage of the product closely by assessing its impact on electronic resources (specifically journals), print collections, and interlibrary loan. The study posited that EDS would increase use of the two former while decreasing the need for document delivery services, which would help justify renewal. Implementation of EDS was found to have increased abstract views and use of EBSCO*host* A&I databases, and there was a 15% growth in e-journal usage. However, there was a strong decrease in use of print material, and that rate of decline was greater than at other libraries in the system that did not have discovery. Effect on document delivery was inconclusive. Decline in print was conjectured to be due to (a) EDS displacing the library catalog as the main search box and (b) the difficulty of finding books in the discovery service through inability to browse by subject, through usage of facets for which books did not have corresponding metadata, and through lack of precision in known item searching (Calvert 2014).

Other libraries report both dramatic increases in database usage and physical item circulation (Faiks, Oberg, and Gabrio 2012; Foster and Williams 2012). Large increases in database usage may be attributed to how they are integrated into the WSD service and how usage data is reported. In EDS, all included EBSCO*host* databases will reflect usage every time that a search is launched. Database recommender services and inclusion of some databases as integrated resources through federated search connectors could also raise user awareness and usage of these sources. Effective integration of print collections in WSD services and boosting of catalog records in search results can bring these resources to users' attention in libraries where the catalog is not being heavily used anymore. As illustrated by West Carolina University, libraries will need to give catalog metadata proper attention and boost and highlight this content whenever possible.

Because central index content will frequently include content and sources to which the library does not already own or subscribe, usage data from the system can help inform purchasing decisions. This is true for individual titles based on COUNTER or link resolver data and for databases and content aggregators. A title's or publisher's presence in the WSD service may also influence purchasing decisions. Montana State University's library reported that it now takes into account whether a publication or subscription source will be searchable in Summon when looking at titles for purchase. It will also encourage vendors/publishers to make their data available in Summon if it is not already, and it will inform vendors/publishers that lack of participation may influence ongoing subscription (Babbit, Foster, and Rossmann 2012). The University of North Florida reported dropping ProQuest databases for EBSCO*host* to increase the reliability of full-text links to those sources when they implemented EDS (Kucsak 2013).

A WSD system may cut into the use of A&I databases, making it appear that they are not as useful in the new environment. Discovery service search boxes that are labeled "one search" or "articles+books" may leave the impression that all the library's resources are included, and users may be less motivated to seek subject-specific databases, which leads to declines in use. The A&I database native interface and content will frequently continue to be an important tool for more sophisticated users and those with subject-specific information needs. Creating integrated resource connections, database recommenders, or other avenues from the WSD service to A&I databases will help to increase user awareness.

Libraries should also be cautious when considering cancellation of e-resource content sources due to lower usage in the WSD interface. There are preliminary studies indicating that some systems may return content from particular sources or publishers more frequently than others (Levine-Clark, MacDonald, and Price 2013). This is discussed further in "Emerging Standards for Web-Scale Discovery" (chapter 12).

Document Delivery

A WSD service will frequently expose users to a greater breadth of content sources. Depending on how system defaults are set, users may encounter more materials that are not immediately available in library collections. This can result in an increase in document delivery/interlibrary loan borrowing activity. At a 2011 ALA presentation, four academic libraries that had implemented WSD systems reported that use of local physical collections declined while ILL borrowing increased (Kemp 2012).

WorldCat Discovery Service is an example of a system that could amplify ILL demand because it includes by default the holdings of other local libraries and allows ILL/document delivery requesting to be conveniently integrated in the search interface. University of Louisville Libraries reported that ILL borrowing for books nearly doubled after WorldCat Local implementation and that they had comments from graduate students and faculty indicating that they appreciated the ease of finding these materials with the system (Goldberg, Johnson, and Kuehn 2012).

When available, setting defaults for full-text or Available in Library content can help reduce the demand for sources not available locally if demand for document delivery services becomes problematic. In WorldCat Discovery Service, libraries can designate a top-tier group of libraries whose holdings display more frequently in search results. This can be customized to include institutions with which the library has reciprocal borrowing arrangements or consortia ties.

Cataloging

> Traditional cataloguing records no longer reside only in each library's local system. The information contained in the records is often extracted and indexed along with other information in federated and aggregated environments, for use both within and outside of an institution. (Han 2012)

Though Han was speaking about a next-generation cataloging environment in her 2012 article examining implications for cataloging, much of what was discussed is relevant to web-scale discovery. The quality of cataloging and metadata in library's local records has become more important in the discovery environment because of the way that this data is exposed and used. A 2011 usability study of a VuFind next-generation catalog revealed how variability of cataloging could negatively affect faceted navigation (Denton and Coysh 2011). Using the same tags consistently to encode data and adhering to controlled vocabularies helps improve facet content and makes records more discoverable.

Han notes that when the 36 top occurring data fields and subfields in MARC were compared with the 25 most used data fields and subfields in a faceted discovery system, there was only a 9-field overlap. When limited to LC's "minimal-level" MARC standard, there were only 3 (Han 2012). That leaves a lot of MARC data unexposed for search and discovery. While libraries using next-generation catalog systems such as VuFind have a good deal of control over which MARC tags will feed certain facets, WSD services vary in degree of customizability. Catalogers should discuss with vendors which tags feed certain fields/facets and make adjustments to local practice if necessary. Calvert attributed lower usage of physical collections after WSD service implementation partly on the fact that LCSH subject terms often do not occur frequently enough in search results in discovery systems to appear in the top 50 displayed in subject facet groups. This makes book content and other MARC record-based content less visible (Calvert 2014). Exploring breaking LCSH out as a separate facet may be a solution, or applying subject terms from other more frequently used thesauri could be considered. For example, health sciences libraries using LCSH instead of the National Library of Medicine's MeSH should consider including MeSH for better exposure.

Another area that may require greater attention is assignment of material-type coding. This generally comes from the Record Type fixed field but could also come from the 245 subfield ‡h. This designation will determine which of the material type icons will be assigned to the record in the search results display. Again, this should be discussed with the vendor during initial system configuration, and catalogers should be alert to check the validity of entries for the field/tag agreed on to deliver this information.

Another impact to cataloging services is the delivery of local records to the service. This is discussed in detail in chapter 7. Delays in catalog record updates to the WSD service may require some changes in cataloging practice to prevent the two systems from getting out of sync. At Grand Valley State University, an early Summon adopter, catalog records are now encoded with a suppressed status for withdrawn items, instead of being immediately removed. This allows the record to be flagged for deletion and sent to Summon as a withdrawal. Suppressed and withdrawn records are now deleted from the integrated library system annually (Daniels and Roth 2012).

In a sea of full-text sources, local library catalog records can be drowned out if they are not boosted by relevancy-ranking algorithms. To aid in discoverability, libraries with WSD services should start to look at methods to deliver more granular metadata. Providing metadata at the chapter level for books, for example, can help improve retrieval in

TEXTBOX 11.2.

CONSIDERATIONS FOR CATALOGERS

- Maximize the value of your data by mapping as much of the MARC and local data fields as possible to existing central index fields and facets.
- Consider adding subject data from other thesauri that matches those used by key central index content.
- Add table of contents and abstracts to local records whenever available.
- Check the validity of mappings regularly to make sure that new fields (RDA) are included.

full-text searches. Han advocates delivering metadata at the individual data-element level, as opposed to the record level, to open records and the data stored within them to more effective query and potentially preserve and make user-contributed data, such as tags and reviews, discoverable (Han 2012). The Library of Congress is moving the library community in the direction of data-level cataloging utilizing RDF and linked data standards with the BIBFRAME project (Library of Congress 2012). This could have important impacts on web-scale discovery in the future. In the meantime, catalogers should look for opportunities to deliver more granular metadata when available.

TEXTBOX 11.3.

RECOMMENDED TASKS FOR OPTIMAL WSD SERVICE MAINTENANCE

1. Monitor usage monthly to ensure that usage levels remain high and there is not significantly less than a 1:1 ratio of full-text views to search sessions.
2. When available, check statistics on most popular searches and top searches with no results to gain insight into areas of weakness and make adjustments to address.
3. Set up Google Analytics for embedded search boxes/widgets to monitor their use.
4. Check the search interface and run test searches regularly to catch unanticipated changes and issues.
5. Test the system thoroughly after any major software updates or changes in content.
6. Subscribe to Listservs, blogs, or Twitter feeds for the user community, and stay in regular touch with the vendor representative assigned to the library's account.
7. Develop relationships with other system subscribers to aid in lobbying for enhancements or new content sources.
8. Document any local customizations or configurations that are important to maintain.
9. Use usage data to aid in collection development decisions, though use caution when basing cancellation decisions on declines in use of native databases or subscription titles postimplementation of WSD.

(continued)

TEXTBOX 11.3. *Continued*

10. Encourage publishers/vendors whose content is not included in the WSD system's central index to become a partner.
11. Monitor document delivery/ILL borrowing levels, and consider making adjustments to the system if activity becomes too burdensome.
12. Make sure that cataloging practices are consistent to properly populate facets and identify correct material types for local holdings.
13. Consider greater granularity in metadata provided for local records to make them more discoverable.
14. Load local records on a regular schedule, and make adjustments in cataloging practice necessary to keep the ILS/catalog in sync with the WSD system.
15. Continue to keep pace with the WSD market to learn about new features and products coming to market or changes in content availability.
16. Take steps to prepare for a switch at the end of the subscription period if another product offers a better potential match for local needs.

Resource Description and Access (RDA), the new cataloging content standard that is finally coming into use, was designed to improve resource discovery in OPACs and other discovery layers. At its heart was a new way of looking at library metadata and record structure. RDA expresses and formalizes relationships among works, entities, manifestations, and items (WEMI). The ability for a user to search at the work level and see all related entities (editions) and manifestations (print vs. electronic) was the vision that developers had in mind. Unfortunately, most discovery products do not yet do a very good job of exploiting these capabilities. This may come as linked data is adopted (see "Integrating Open Linked Data and Altmetrics," chapter 12). For now, catalogers should be aware of the new tags being introduced by RDA and make sure that the metadata gets mapped to appropriate indexes.

Keeping Up with the Changing Market

The web-scale discovery market is dynamic. Products are constantly undergoing change, and new products could be coming to the market to compete with the four currently established. In the past year, hybrid systems combining discovery layers from next-generation catalogs and content from EDS were released. Changes in the content landscape can also effect which system will be the best match for a library. A publisher or aggregator may choose to withdraw content from a particular system, or a new content source may become exclusively available through a competitor system. Keeping up with developments is important for those shopping for a system and those who currently have one.

Because WSD products are offered by annual subscription, libraries have the option of making a change at the end of the subscription year if they are unhappy with their current service. Libraries that are considering making a move should take steps well in advance of the end of the subscription year to prepare, including content analysis and customization, trialing, and usability testing. There may need to be an overlap in the two subscriptions to allow sufficient time to configure the new system and build new search boxes/widgets.

The following sources and websites are recommended to stay on top of an ever-changing discovery landscape.

ALA Tech Source Publications

http://www.alatechsource.org. The ALA Tech Source site provides links to several technology-focused publications and the ALA Tech Source blog. *Library Technology Reports* issues focus on a particular technology and provide in-depth analysis and summaries of products. Jason Vaughan reported on web-scale discovery in the winter 2011 issue, which was devoted to the topic. Marshall Breeding authored the winter 2014 issue, on resource discovery services, which also looks at web-scale discovery products in detail. LTR full-text content is available by subscription or purchase. *Smart Libraries Newsletter* is written by Marshall Breeding and reports on developments in the library technology world and vendor news. Much of the content is also available via Breeding's Library Technology Guides website (see below).

Library Technology Reports: http://www.alatechsource.org/ltr/index

Smart Libraries Newsletter: http://www.alatechsource.org/sln/index

TEXTBOX 11.4.

TWITTER FEEDS TO FOLLOW

@ALA_TechSource: ALA Tech Source, "American Library Association imprint for librarian geeks and technology innovators. Regular contributors include Dan Freeman and Patrick Hogan."

@EBSCO: EBSCO Information Services official company feed.

@ExLibrisGroup: Ex Libris official company feed.

@LibraryJournal: Library Journal, "Library views, news, and book reviews from *LJ* staffers."

@mbreeding: Marshall Breeding—"Independent consultant, Speaker, and Author; editor of *Library Technology Guides,* columnist for *Computers in Libraries,* Editor of *Smart Libraries Newsletter.*"

@OCLC: OCLC official company feed.

@ProQuest: ProQuest official company feed.

@ShiftTheDigital: The Digital Shift "On Libraries and New Media, powered by—@LibraryJournal and @SLJournal | Tweets by@BarbaraAGenco."

@varnum: Ken Varnum "Libraries, Discovery, Drupal and More."

InformationToday

http://www.infotoday.com. InformationToday publishes monthly issues of *Information-Today*, which contains newsy articles on the information industry, including library technology vendors. Several other InfoToday publications cover library automation and searching/discovery services, including *Computers in Libraries*, *Online Searcher*, and *Online*. A Weekly News Break service makes summaries of articles that will be featured in upcoming issues available for free.

NewsBreaks/Weekly News Digests: newsbreaks.infotoday.com

Library Journal

http://www.libraryjournal.com. Library Journal frequently reports on library technology and breaking product news from library vendors. It has frequently reported in the past two years on web-scale discovery. Check "The Digital Shift" section for technology-focused news. Free weekly e-newsletters, *LJXpress* and *Academic Newswire*, are available to receive summaries of the week's news via e-mail. *Library Journal* also offers free webcasts focusing on new technologies and products. These are often cosponsored by vendors:

The Digital Shift: http://www.thedigitalshift.com

LJXpress and Academic Newswire Subscription: http://lj.libraryjournal.com/newsletters/

LJ Webcasts: http://lj.libraryjournal.com/category/webcasts/

Library Technology Guides

http://www.librarytechnology.org. Marshall Breeding—a consultant, speaker, and author, and formerly of Vanderbilt University Libraries—writes frequently about library automation trends. In the past 10 years, he has also focused on next-generation catalogs and discovery services. Breeding currently serves on the NISO Open Discovery Initiative Working Group and was a founding member. His Library Technology Guides website hosts his GuidePosts blog and his annual Perceptions survey report on library automation. Also found on LTG:

Annual Automation Marketplace Report: Usually published in *Library Journal* in April, it details the major library automation vendors, their products, and sales figures.

Discovery Layer Interfaces: http://www.librarytechnology.org/discovery.pl; provides links to most of the discovery layer and WSD products currently on the market and includes a list of subscribing libraries.

Library Companies: http://www.librarytechnology.org/companies.pl; lists all the major vendors, including all the companies currently offering WSD products. Profiles of each vendor include contact information and links to all press releases issued by the company since it began being profiled.

Key Points

Libraries that purchase WSD services should closely monitor system usage statistics to assess impacts to use of the library's electronic resources and improvements in user search experience. These can help justify the system by demonstrating return on investment. A low ratio of views/downloads of full-text documents to search sessions may indicate that the system is not returning useful results or full-text results are not easy to retrieve.

Because these systems are in a constant state of change and development, subscribing libraries should monitor systems closely, particularly after major software upgrades. Documenting local settings and customizations will help restore them quickly if disabled by an update. System administrators and those who support user search activities should subscribe to Listservs, Twitter feeds, or other methods of communication from the vendor to stay informed of major developments.

Having a WSD system can affect collection development, document delivery, and cataloging practices. Though WSD systems generally increase the use of electronic collections, impacts on other database products and print collections are mixed and largely dependent on the local environment, the system purchased, and configuration decisions. Document delivery and ILL demands can increase but may be moderated by applying Available in Library or full-text-only defaults or boosting results from libraries that extend reciprocal borrowing. Catalogers will need to pay close attention to consistency in cataloging practice and may want to adopt granular/data-level cataloging to expose more metadata for discovery.

The WSD market is constantly evolving. Libraries that are shopping for WSD products or have already purchased one are encouraged to closely monitor new products and features coming to market. Since most WSD services are offered as yearly subscriptions, libraries can make a change if desired at the end of the subscription term.

References

Babbit, Elizabeth P., Amy Foster, and Doralyn Rossmann. 2012. "Implementation of Resource Discovery: Lessons Learned." In *Planning and Implementing Resource Discovery Tools in Academic Libraries*, edited by Mary Pagliero Popp and Diane Dallis, 580–97. Hershey, PA: IGI Global.

Calvert, Kristin. 2014. "Maximizing Academic Library Collections: Measuring Changes in Use Patterns Owing to EBSCO Discovery Service." *College and Research Libraries*. http://crl.acrl.org/content/early/2014/01/17/crl13-557.full.pdf+html.

Daniels, Jeffrey, and Patrick Roth. 2012. "Incorporating Millennium Catalog Records into Serials Solutions' Summon." *Technical Services Quarterly* 29, no. 3: 193–99.

Denton, William, and Sarah J. Coysh. 2011. "Usability Testing of VuFind at an Academic Library." *Library Hi Tech* 29, no. 2: 301–19.

Faiks, Angi, Johnan Oberg, and Katy Gabrio. 2012. "WorldCat Local: A Transformative Solution." In *Planning and Implementing Resource Discovery Tools in Academic Libraries*, edited by Mary Pagliero Popp and Diane Dallis, 608–21. Hershey, PA: IGI Global.

Foster, Anita K., and Sarah C. Williams. 2012. "Early Adoption: EBSCO Discovery Service at Illinois State University." In *Planning and Implementing Resource Discovery Tools in Academic Libraries*, edited by Mary Pagliero Popp and Diane Dallis, 488–98. Hershey, PA: IGI Global.

Goldberg, Tyler, Anna Marie Johnson, and Randy Kuehn. 2012. "Tiptoeing Forward: Implementing and Integrating WorldCat Local as a Discovery Tool." In *Planning and Implementing Resource Discovery Tools in Academic Libraries*, edited by Mary Pagliero Popp and Diane Dallis, 622–33. Hershey, PA: IGI Global.

Han, Myung-Ja. 2012. "New Discovery Services and Library Bibliographic Control." *Library Trends* 61, no. 1: 162–72.

Hoeppner, Athena. 2013. "Zen and the Art of WSD Maintenance." *Web-Scale Discovery Services: Transforming Access to Library Resources.* NISO virtual conference. November 20. http://www.niso.org/news/events/2013/virtual/discovery/#slides.

Kemp, Jan. 2012. "Does Web-Scale Discovery Make a Difference? Changes in Collections Use after Implementing Summon." In *Planning and Implementing Resource Discovery Tools in Academic Libraries*, edited by Mary Pagliero Popp and Diane Dallis, 456–68. Hershey, PA: IGI Global.

Kucsak, Michael. 2013. "Delivering the Goods." *Web-Scale Discovery Services: Transforming Access to Library Resources.* NISO virtual conference. November 20. http://www.niso.org/news/events/2013/virtual/discovery/#slides.

Levine-Clark, Michael, John MacDonald, and Jason Price. 2013. "Discovery or Displacement: A Large Scale Institutional Study of the Effect of Discovery Systems on Online Journal Usage." Paper presented at the Charleston Conference, Charleston, SC. http://2013charlestonconference.sched.org/event/303dfa600e13ba7c339e2461f127a667#.Unuqh_msiM5.

Library of Congress. 2012. "Bibliographic Framework as a Web of Data: Linked Data Model and Supporting Services." November 21. http://www.loc.gov/bibframe/pdf/marcld-report-11-21-2012.pdf.

Way, Doug. 2010. "The Impact of Web-Scale Discovery on the Use of a Library Collection." *Serials Review* 36 (August): 214–20.

CHAPTER 12

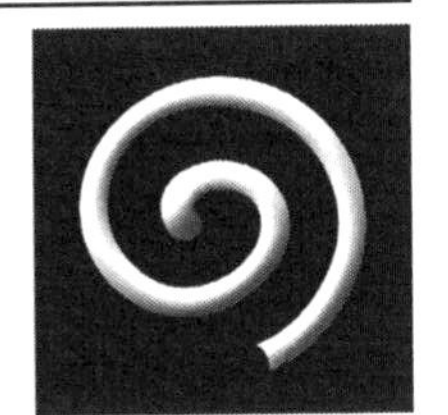

The Future of Web-Scale Discovery

IN THIS CHAPTER

- ▷ Emerging Standards for Web-Scale Discovery
- ▷ Moving toward a More Equitable Content Environment
- ▷ Personalizing the Search Experience for Users
- ▷ Improving Access to Print Materials and E-books
- ▷ Integrating Open Linked Data and Altmetrics

Emerging Standards for Web-Scale Discovery

About a year after the launches of EDS and Primo Central, the need for standards to define what these emerging new discovery services were and to establish best practices was first discussed formally at ALA 2011 in New Orleans. This initial meeting—led by Oren Beit-Arie and Jenny Walker of Ex Libris and Marshall Breeding of Library Technology Guides—laid the groundwork for establishing the Open Discovery Initiative (ODI). The ODI is a working group of the National Information Standards Organization (NISO), which provides a neutral forum for vendors, content providers, and libraries. ODI Working Group members include academic librarians, representatives from publishers and other content providers, and discovery service vendors.

> The Open Discovery Initiative aims to facilitate increased transparency in the content coverage of index-based discovery services and to recommend consistent methods of content exchange or other mechanisms. Full transparency will enable libraries to objectively evaluate discovery services and to deal with daily operational issues surrounding these products. (NISO Open Discovery Initiative Working Group 2013c)

This call for standards was in the wake of growing concerns about WSD subscribers' abilities to discern just how much of their full-text electronic content was available in any given discovery service and the level of metadata available for covered sources. Content providers were also concerned about how their data was being indexed and discovered in WSD services, with some (e.g., the American Chemical Society) refusing to contribute full-text content to any of the services. Differing levels of available metadata may leave important resources undiscovered or buried deep in search results (Kelley 2012).

Preliminary results of the first large-scale study on the effects of discovery systems on electronic resource usage were reported at the Charleston Conference in October 2013 and indicate that differing levels of metadata, relevance-ranking algorithms, and linking/routing practices may make an impact on discovery and usage of individual content sources. The study analyzed usage of four major academic publishers at 24 libraries that had implemented one of the four WSD services (EDS, Primo, Summon, or WorldCat Local). COUNTER statistics a year pre- and postimplementation of WSD were compared. Initial analysis indicated that discovery tools could affect the usage of particular publishers, with variability being found among the four WSD services (Levine-Clark, MacDonald, and Price 2013). These findings highlight the need for further transparency and a better understanding of how relevancy ranking, linking, and varying metadata levels influence discovery.

At the same time that the ODI was being formed, content providers and database producers began an initiative through the National Federation of Advanced Information Services (NFAIS) to also formulate best practices. The NFAIS published a document in 2013 titled "Recommended Practices: Discovery Services":

> Acceptance of these Recommended Practices will help facilitate full disclosure and transparency for the ultimate benefit of information seekers so that they will be able to know the parameters of the information that they are searching and to which they have access, and to become aware of the complex relationships among the participants in any Discovery Service arrangement.

The NFAIS document defines what a discovery service is, identifies the five participants in a service (content owner, platform that provides the content, discovery service, discovery service subscriber, and user), and creates a matrix of the five participants, identifying each one's rights and obligations. For example, "inclusion of only contractually agreed upon content" is a right of the content owner and an obligation of the discovery service (NFAIS 2013).

The ODI/NISO initiative will be more in depth and is still a work in progress, though great strides have been made in the past year. The goals are to address the following issues:

- "Create ways for libraries to assess the level of content providers' participation in discovery services."
- "Help streamline the process by which content providers work with discovery service vendors."
- "Define models for fair or unbiased linking from discovery services to publishers' content."
- "Determine what usage statistics should be collected." (NISO Open Discovery Initiative Group 2013c)

In 2012, the ODI conducted a survey of librarians, content providers, and discovery service providers to gather data about discovery services and what libraries require from them, including metadata delivery and indexing, methods of data exchange, and usage data provision and needs. The results provide a window into the adoption and use of discovery services in libraries. There were 871 respondents, with the majority being librarians. Of the librarian respondents, 74% indicated that their institution had implemented a discovery service, but this may be skewed by the fact that those motivated to complete the survey were more likely to have a discovery service. According to survey findings, librarians want to be able to compare the coverage offered by a discovery service to their holdings, with ability to compare at the title level preferred rather than at the collection level. They also want to offer "broad flexibility in search results, in order to serve a range of users." Being able to get users to full text quickly was of high priority, and librarians want to be able to control the link resolver configuration, with preference to link the user to the native publisher interface whenever possible (NISO Open Discovery Initiative Group 2013b).

Based on the survey results, *Promoting Transparency in Discovery: A Recommended Practice of the National Information Standards Organization* was put forward for public comment in October 2013 (NISO Open Discovery Initiative Group 2013c). Among the general recommendations was a call for content providers to contribute to all discovery services and provide a minimum defined set of metadata for indexing. This metadata is shown in table 12.1. The document also established the metadata elements necessary to label it as "enhanced metadata." Content providers were requested to disclose specifically what sources and metadata were being sent to the discovery services.

General recommendations for discovery service providers were to

- annually publish a statement of nonbias with regard to content indexed and results presented to the user,
- provide recommended usage reports to participating content providers and library customers, and
- offer library customers discovery service content listings.

The document put forward recommendations for ensuring transparency and fair practices for linking, data transmission and indexing, and relevancy-ranking algorithms. It also made recommendations for minimal usage data to be generated and made available to both content providers and subscribers monthly. For subscribers, these include

Table 12.1. Basic Data Elements to Be Provided by Content Providers

ELEMENT NAME	DESCRIPTION
Title	Main title of the item
Print identifier	One or more standard numbers for the print version (OCLC #, ISBN, ISSN, etc.)
Online identifier	One or more of the standard numbers for the online version (DOI, ISBN, ISSN, etc.)
Date	The date of publication. For a serial run, the date of the first issue
Item URL	OpenURL or a direct link for the item's full-text
Authors	The author(s) of the item
Publisher Name	The name of the publisher

total number of searches, total number of unique visitors, number of click-throughs to full text, top 500 search queries, and top 100 referring URLs. It recommended that these metrics be available in COUNTER and that further integration with COUNTER be explored.

A second document of recommended guidelines concerning open-access metadata was released in late 2013 with a comment period that ended in February 2014. The purpose of this document was to develop metadata standards for open-access content and reuse rights, which should assist discovery service providers and users in providing both access to and use of this content (NISO Open Discovery Initiative Users Group 2013a).

The group will continue to develop standards and "develop mechanisms to evaluate conformance with the Recommended Practice" (NISO Open Discovery Initiative Users Group 2013c). Conformance with these emerging standards will provide another important evaluation factor when libraries are selecting and purchasing WSD services in the future.

Moving toward a More Equitable Content Environment

Competition among the WSD service vendors has created an environment of inequity when it comes to available content. Being able to market as the exclusive vendor of particular content sources gives a vendor an edge. It also puts libraries that require this content in a bad position. If they want this content included in their WSD service, they have only one viable option to choose from.

In May 2013, the Orbis Cascade Alliance, a large consortium of college and university libraries in the Northwest, issued a letter to Ex Libris and EBSCO requesting that all their subscribed EBSCO database content be accessible for discovery in their Primo service:

> We believe that it is reasonable to expect the inclusion of EBSCO databases as distinct collections in the Primo Central Index supplying metadata to Primo. Our members are heavily invested in EBSCO content and each member should be able to selectively access the databases they have purchased. . . .
>
> We urge EBSCO and Ex Libris to quickly resolve this issue. Failure to do so is a disservice to your customers and the faculty, students, and researchers we serve. Left unresolved, we will be required to reconsider the shape and scope of future business with EBSCO and Ex Libris. (Orbis Cascade Alliance 2013)

The letter and the responses from the two companies were posted to the Orbis Cascade Alliance's website, where any interested party could access them. Ex Libris responded that it had an agreement to index "comprehensive metadata" for several key EBSCO databases in 2009 but that the agreement was ended by EBSCO in 2010 when EDS launched. According to Ex Libris, the two companies had not been able to reach an agreement since (Ex Libris 2013b). In its letter, EBSCO said that it had offered Ex Libris API access to EBSCO content, which Ex Libris rejected. EBSCO claims in this document that API access is superior to providing the metadata for inclusion in Primo Central's central index and that it does not have the right to provide this content, which belongs to third-party database providers. EBSCO goes on to say that the "providers are concerned that the relevancy ranking algorithm in Primo

Central does not take advantage of the value added elements of their products and thus would result in lower usage of their databases and a diminished user experience for researchers" (EBSCO 2013).

Ex Libris countered all of these arguments in an open letter to the library community:

- "The content they are seeking is content owned by EBSCO."
- "The API is to EDS, not EBSCOhost, forcing EBSCOhost subscribers who want to access this content via Primo to also pay for EDS."
- "EDS is an index based search product. Claiming API to be superior seems to be a contradiction of EBSCO practice." (Ex Libris 2013a)

At this point, the two parties remain at an impasse. Ex Libris, being the only WSD service vendor that is not also an aggregator or content provider, is the most vulnerable to the inequities of the current content wars. It is no coincidence that they were founding members of the NISO Open Discovery Initiative, which is addressing many of these issues head-on. But the mere existence of standards calling for even-handed distribution of content metadata to all the discovery services will not change the landscape by itself. More large and influential consortiums and libraries will need to join the Orbis Cascade Alliance in calling for change, and they will need to be willing to pull the plug on content providers and vendors who do not want to accommodate subscribers.

Personalizing the Search Experience for Users

Because WSD services contain such a large pool of content for users to search, the library's ability to customize a service to the needs of its users is critical. But most libraries must account for the needs of a wide range of users. Within academic libraries, the searching needs and habits of undergraduate students vary widely from the needs of faculty researchers. In public libraries, the information needs of adult users are quite different from the needs of school students using library resources to complete homework assignments. The next logical step for these services is to be able to recognize and accommodate the individual user, providing a search interface tailored to the individual's needs.

> The user context is a multidimensional matrix encompassing: (1) level of experience, (2) comprehensiveness of their research need, (3) type of scholarly materials the user primarily works with, (4) user discipline, and also (5) what physical or virtual location the user is performing their research from. (Dehmlow 2013)

Though Dehmlow was talking about academics, many of these factors apply to library users outside academic research environments. The ability for these systems to recognize and respond to needs for particular material types, subject areas, scholarly/grade level, and the user's location/device platform will greatly enhance the user experience.

Most of the WSD services allow users to create accounts and save lists of search results and particular search strategies. Many also allow users to save particular settings that can help tailor the search environment. Summon has a discipline-scoped search environment that can be applied, and it allows users to build personally scoped search boxes and widgets. But much more could be done to make these adjustments automatically. Amazon and Netflix use data about past searches and purchases to suggest certain results to the user. Google has also been tailoring search results to users based on past activities since 2009. Personalization increases relevancy when user searches are short and ambiguous (Davis 2011). Remembering what a logged-in user has searched in the past, what filters have been applied, and what types of material have been viewed could be used similarly by WSD services. Libraries will need to consider impacts on user privacy in this type of environment.

Being able to provide responsive interfaces to adjust to the user's location and access device will also become increasingly important. WSD services will need to be able to provide tailored search environments to allow users to search effectively from smaller devices. When the service is accessed via larger screens, richer environments with more services and features can be presented. The ability to recognize if the user is outside the validated IP range and to offer LDAP or log-in options based on location is also key in mobile environments and when users are accessing services away from the library. As contextually aware search technologies evolve, software will be able to adapt and suggest actions to users based on location or what they are doing. In the future, a WSD service might pop up a floor plan to the library's stacks to show the location of the item if it senses that the user is in the vicinity. Again, these services will have privacy considerations.

Improving Access to Print Materials and E-books

Many libraries that implement web-scale discovery have not been able to entirely do away with a separate OPAC. Frequently WSD services do not provide the ability to place holds on materials, renew checked out items, or view and pay fines owed. Any of these library user account activities still have to be done in the OPAC. The WSD service will provide a link to the OPAC from the bibliographic record, but from there the user is in another interface, sometimes having to log-in a second time. Similarly, requests to borrow print materials from outside the library's collections also require a link out to whatever system the library is using to manage ILL transactions.

WSD services could do a better job of integrating these activities directly into the WSD interface. SIP and SIP2 standards already exist for sending user account information that resides in the ILS to self-service vendors such as 3M and mobile services vendors such as Boopsie for managing circulation transactions (renewals, hold placement, and fine payment). The Digital Library Federation (DLF) issued recommendations for API to extract circulation and user account information from integrated library systems for use in discovery layers in 2008 (DLF ILS Discovery Interface Task Group 2008). These could be used to bring circulation and user account functions directly into the WSD service, cutting out the intervening OPAC layer altogether. Summon is building toward this functionality with the integration of patron holds, and OCLC's new WorldCat Discovery Services promises to deliver an integrated interlibrary loan function.

E-book loan management is another area where the user needs to leave the WSD service once the item has been discovered. Actually viewing and downloading the content typically happens in the e-book vendor's management interface. As more public libraries subscribe to WSD services, the need to better accommodate e-book discovery and access should result in the services providing this functionality.

In his editorial about services and user context in WSD systems, Dehmlow (2013) mentions the need to be able to build connections among elements in their vast indexes. Bringing additional data about retrieved items—including editorial reviews, user ratings and comments from social media sources, and data about the author—together in the full record view would greatly enhance the content. Embracing evolving linked data technologies will be the key to making this possible.

Google, Bing, Yandex, and other commercial search engines are rapidly adopting linked data in the form of schema.org and using it to bring more content in context to the searcher. Google's Knowledge Graphs present this data in an attractive graphic package, utilizing information and images from Wikipedia and other open-access sources. To continue to compete effectively with commercial search engines, WSD services will need to do the same.

OCLC is already making great strides in the use of linked data to bring this information together and make it accessible to the user. Both WorldCat and WorldCat Discovery Service provide knowledge cards about authors, displaying publication timelines, biographical information, and links to other publications. Part of the knowledge card for Mark Twain is shown in figure 12.1. All WorldCat records now include schema.org markup, which makes it possible to create linkages among records based on the metadata. It also creates pathways for users from the commercial search engines into data and records in WorldCat.

Though most library data continues to be organized at the bibliographic record level, the linked data movement will mean that users will increasingly be searching at the individual data element level and cataloging will be done at this level as well. The Library of Congress's BIBFRAME project is creating an encoding structure that will embrace linked data and resource description framework (RDF) standards, which it envisions

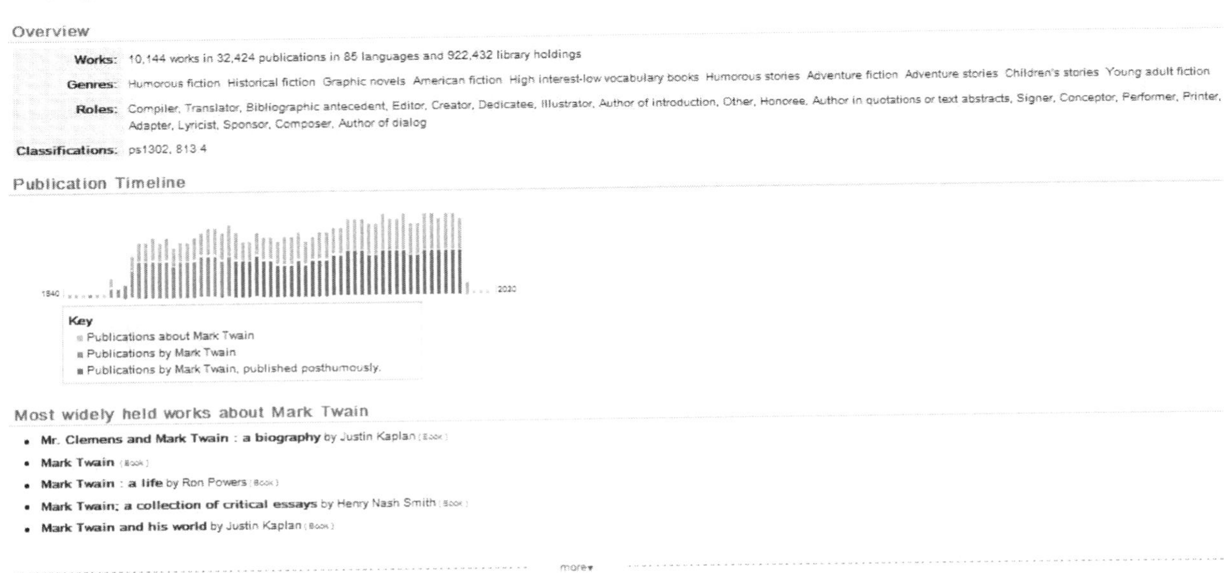

Figure 12.1. WorldCat Knowledge Card for Mark Twain. *© 2014 OCLC Online Computer Library Center, Inc., used with OCLC's permission; WorldCat, WorldCat.org, and the WorldCat logo are registered trademarks/service marks of OCLC.*

will replace MARC in the not-too-distant future. This reorganization at a more granular level will make it easier for users to search for and retrieve data across multiple platforms. There is an argument that WSD services will no longer be necessary in a linked data environment in which commercial search engines will be able to thoroughly exploit these new paths to content and provide further value added, especially as more content becomes open access (Askey 2013; Tay 2013). For now, WSD services will need to be able to keep pace with search engines in embracing and adopting these new technologies and standards.

Altmetrics is also likely to play a role in WSD systems in the future. EBSCO announced the acquisition of Plum Analytics, an alternative research metrics provider, at the 2014 ALA midwinter conference (EBSCO 2014). Plum Analytics will remain an independent subsidiary, but the acquisition signals the increased importance of this type of data analysis for companies such as EBSCO that provide research-focused databases and discovery interfaces. Plum Analytics gathers metrics across five categories; usage, mentions, social media, citations, and captures. This can provide researchers and publishers with more robust data on their impact than can traditional citation analysis alone. Displaying these metrics about a journal article author, for example, could enhance the content WSD searchers retrieve. WSD vendors can also use these metrics as factors in relevancy-ranking algorithms.

Key Points

The landscape continues to change rapidly for web-scale discovery services. Currently, the NISO Open Discovery Initiative is devising standards for discovery services to improve transparency in content holdings and metadata, ranking algorithms, and linking practices. The current content wars among discovery vendors have created an environment of inequity that needs to be challenged by these standard initiatives and library subscribers.

To continue to compete with commercial search engines, WSD services should make efforts to customize the search experience for individual searchers. Bringing services such as managing holds and renewals for print items, as well as downloading and managing e-book lending, directly into the WSD interface will also improve the user experience. Linked data should be incorporated to bring more content in context to the searcher and improve granularity in metadata and searching. Altmetrics may also play a role in enhancing content and refining relevancy-ranking algorithms.

References

Askey, Dale. 2013. "Giving Up on Discovery." *Taiga Forum*. Blog. September 17. http://taiga-forum.org/giving-up-on-discovery/.

Davis, Corey. 2011. "Relevancy Redacted: Web-Scale Discovery and the 'Filter Bubble.'" *Proceedings of the Charleston Library Conference*. http://dx.doi.org/10.5703/1288284314965.

Dehmlow, Mark. 2013. "Services and User Context in the Era of Webscale Discovery." *Information Technology and Libraries* 32, no. 2: 1–3.

DLF ILS Discovery Interface Task Group. 2008. "ILS-DI Technical Recommendation: An API for the Effective Interoperation Between Integrated Library Systems and External Discovery Applications." December 8. http://old.diglib.org/architectures/ilsdi/DLF_ILS_Discovery_1.1.doc.

EBSCO. 2013. "EBSCO Response to Alliance Board, May 8, 2013." http://www.orbiscascade.org/index/ebsco-and-ex-libris.

———. 2014. "Plum Analytics Becomes Part of EBSCO Information Services." Press release. January 14. http://www.ebscohost.com/newsroom/stories/plum-analytics-becomes-part-of-ebsco-information-services.

Ex Libris. 2013a. "Ex Libris Open Letter to the Library Community, May 14, 2013." http://www.orbiscascade.org/index/ebsco-and-ex-libris.

———. 2013b. "Ex Libris Response to Alliance Board, May 6, 2013." http://www.orbiscascade.org/index/ebsco-and-ex-libris.

Kelley, Michael. 2012. "Coming into Focus: Web-Scale Discovery Services Face Growing Need for Best Practices." *Library Journal* 137, no. 17: 34.

Levine-Clark, Michael, John MacDonald, and Jason Price. 2013. "Discovery or Displacement: A Large Scale Institutional Study of the Effect of Discovery Systems on Online Journal Usage." Paper presented at the Charleston Conference, Charleston, SC. November 7. http://2013charlestonconference.sched.org/event/303dfa600e13ba7c339e2461f127a667#.Unuqh_msiM5.

National Federation of Advanced Information Services (NFAIS). 2013. "Recommended Practices: Discovery Services." August 30. http://info.nfais.org/info/Recommended_Practices_Final_Aug_2013.pdf.

NISO Open Discovery Initiative Working Group. 2013a. *Open Access Metadata and Indicators.* Baltimore, MD: National Information Standards Organization.

———. 2013b. "ODI Survey Report: Reflections and Perspectives on Discovery Services." January. http://www.niso.org/apps/group_public/download.php/9977/NISO%20ODI%20Survey%20Report%20Final.pdf.

———. 2013c. *Promoting Transparency in Discovery: A Recommended Practice of the National Information Standards Organization.* Baltimore, MD: National Information Standards Organization.

Orbis Cascade Alliance. 2013. "Alliance Board Letter to EBSCO and Ex Libris, May 2, 2013." http://www.orbiscascade.org/index/ebsco-and-ex-libris.

Tay, Aaron. 2013. "The Day Library Discovery Died—2035." *Musings about Librarianship.* Blog. September 22. http://musingsaboutlibrarianship.blogspot.com/2013/09/the-day-library-discovery-died-2035.html#.UsxvJvRDuSo.

Appendix: Sample Features Table for Scoring Web-Scale Discovery Systems

The following table can be used as a checklist and evaluative tool to ensure that desired features and functionality are available and to measure one product against another. Libraries can customize it by removing features that are not required or adding desired features or functionality not included. Assign the vendor score based on the priority and availability of the feature. For example, if boosting of local records is a highly desired element that the system has, the product score is a 3. The product score is a 0 for any desired feature that is not available.

WSD SYSTEM FEATURE	REQUIRED—3	HIGHLY DESIRED—2	DESIRED—1	PRODUCT SCORE	NOTES
Customizable facet groups					
Adjustable relevancy ranking					
Boosting of local (catalog) records					
Ability to turn content sources on or off					
Integration of databases and content not covered in central index					
Limit to full text retrieval only					
Limit to remove newspaper content					
Limit to academic or peer reviewed journals					
Recommender services					
Spell checking					
Known item searching					
Search history display					
Personalized folders					
Shared folders					
Save searches					
RSS feeds					
E-mail results/alerts					
Persistent links					
Citation save					

Citation export					
User tags					
User reviews					
Library mediation for tags and reviews					
Book jacket images					
Customizable publication type icons					
Multilingual screens and help					
Full-text language translation					
Composite catalog record (FRBR)					
Merged record de-duping					
IP range authentication					
EZproxy authentication					
LDAP or Shibboleth authentication					
Guest access					
Mobile apps for Apple and Android					
Responsive mobile					
Integrated OPAC services (renews, holds)					
Multiple profiles for multilibrary installations					
Display of multilibrary holdings for catalog records					
Documentation and support for API					
Total for X Product					

Glossary

A&I databases—Subject- or discipline-focused databases that include indexing and abstracts for books, chapters, journals, and magazine content. The strength of A&I databases is the specificity of searching using the assigned index terms.

Aggregator—The organization that collects information from varied sources and provides consistent search, presentation, and/or access (NISO Open Discovery Initiative Working Group 2013).

Altmetrics (alternative research metrics)—Metrics that are an alternative to traditional citation impact measures, including journal impact factors. Altmetrics utilizes article views, downloads, or mentions in social and news media to measure the impact of people, journals, books, webpages, and so on (adapted from Wikipedia 2014).

Android—An operating system based on Linux for mobile devices. Android, Inc., the initial developer, was bought out by Google. It is the most popular mobile OS in the United States. Unlike Apple's iOS, which powers iPhone devices, Google makes Android code available as open source to developers. Android is also used in televisions, digital cameras, and gaming systems.

API (application programming interface)—"A language and message format used by an application program to communicate with the operating system or some other control program such as a database management system (DBMS) or communications protocol. APIs are implemented by writing function calls in the program, which provide the linkage to the required subroutine for execution" (*PC Magazine Encyclopedia* 2014). A system with an API interface is said to be "open" because it provides a method to easily pass data to other programs and services. "Read" APIs allow data to be passed to another service, while "write" APIs allow manipulation of the data.

Bibliographic Framework Initiative (BIBFRAME)—An initiative of the Library of Congress to develop an RDF-based model for expressing and connecting bibliographic data. The goal of the BIBFRAME initiative is to develop a new standard that will replace MARC for encoding bibliographic metadata. More information is available at http://www.loc.gov/bibframe/.

Browser—"Client software that interprets the hypertext (HTML) code in which Web pages are written and allows documents and other data files available over the Internet to be viewed in graphical, as opposed to text-only, format" (Reitz 2014). Common browser software includes IE (Internet Explorer) for Microsoft Windows, Google Chrome, Mozilla Firefox, and Safari for MacIntosh and iPhone. Other mobile devices commonly use Opera and Opera Mini.

Cascading style sheets—Also known as CSS, cascading style sheets is HTML-based code that designates the colors, fonts, and other design elements that are to be included on all pages of a website.

Central Index—"The central index (also called a 'unified index') is a collection of content that is systematically harvested from diverse sources, such as journal publishers, database producers, library catalogs and collections, open-source full text, repositories, and so on. The harvested content is then processed and preindexed to facilitate quick searching" (NFAIS 2013).

CJK—"It is a commonly used acronym for 'Chinese, Japanese, and Korean.' The term 'CJK character' generally refers to 'Chinese characters,' or more specifically, the Chinese (= Han) ideographs used in the writing systems of the Chinese and Japanese languages, occasionally for Korean, and historically in Vietnam" (Unicode Consortium 2014).

Cloud Based (also Cloud Computing)—Subscription or pay-per-use services, including SaaS, hosted services, platform as a service, or virtual server services that exist outside an organization's local network or an individual's local hardware and are accessed in real time over the Internet. They extend computing capacity without requiring direct local infrastructure or support.

Connector—A code-based tool to access and search a remote data source using connection protocols such as Z39.50 and OAI. Connectors are utilized by federated and metasearch services to search and identify retrieval from databases and other content sources.

Content Aggregator—"A content aggregator is an organization that licenses content (e.g., journals, databases) from diverse sources for subscription and distribution via that organization's own proprietary search and delivery platform" (NFAIS 2013).

Content Provider—"These organizations offer content products or services, primarily intended for access by library patrons or the general public. The content provided by these organizations is used to generate the central indexes associated with the discovery services. Content providers include commercial and non-profit organizations" (NISO Open Discovery Initiative Working Group 2013).

Contentdm—A digital collections management tool from OCLC. It stores and can be used to edit data and images. It is also used to upload metadata of digital contents to WorldCat. More information is available at http://www.oclc.org/en-US/contentdm/overview.html.

COUNTER (Counting Online Usage of Networked Electronic Resources)—An international initiative serving librarians, publishers, and intermediaries by setting standards that facilitate the recording and reporting of online usage statistics in a consistent, credible, and compatible way (NISO 2013).

De-duping—Removing duplicate bibliographic records from a retrieval list. A bibliographic item may be included as a record in several content sources in a WSD service. A search may retrieve these "duplicate" records for the same items. Some systems include a means to identify and remove multiple records for the same item or merge the records to display the unique bibliographic information from each.

Digital Library Federation (DLF)—A program of the Council on Library and Information Resources, the DLF promotes work on digital library standards and best practices. The organization's ILS Discovery Interface Task Group issued recommendations for API to extract circulation and user account information from integrated library systems for use in the discovery layer in 2008. More information is available at http://old.diglib.org/architectures/ilsdi/DLF_ILS_Discovery_1.1.doc.

Discovery Layer—The user interface and search system for discovering, displaying, and interacting with the content in library systems, such as a WSD central index (Hoeppner 2012).

Dublin Core—A standard set of 15 metadata elements for resource description. Dublin Core includes traditional bibliographic descriptive elements such as title, subject, and publisher, but it also includes concepts such as "relation" and "rights." Dublin Core can be encoded in XML, HTML, and RDF. More information at http://www.niso.org/apps/group_public/download.php/10256/Z39-85-2012_dublin_core.pdf.

EAD (encoded archival description)—An XML standard for encoding archival finding aids, which originated at the University of California at Berkeley in 1993 and is maintained by the Technical Subcommittee for Encoded Archival Description of the Society of American Archivists, in partnership with the Library of Congress. More information at http://www.loc.gov/ead.

EBSCO*host*—The searching interface for subscription databases that EBSCO Information Services hosts for publishers and content providers.

Enriched Content—Jacket images, table of contents, summaries, and reviews supplied from a subscription source such as Syndetics or Content Café. This content enhances the information that displays for a bibliographic record in a WSD service.

EZproxy—A widely used authentication service sold by OCLC, it authenticates library users against local authentication systems and provides remote access to licensed content based on the user's authorization.

Facets—Categories derived from content metadata that provide the searcher with options to narrow search results. A subject facet allows the searcher to limit search results to just records assigned a particular subject index term.

Federated Search—"Federated search is an information retrieval technology that allows the simultaneous search of multiple searchable resources. A user makes a single query request which is distributed to the search engines participating in the federation. The federated search then aggregates the results that are received from the search engines for presentation to the user" (Wikipedia 2014). Most library federated search systems use the Z39.50 protocol. Federated search is also known as metasearch.

Filters (in this context, the same as limiter)—Filters allow searchers to select a subset of the resources available in a search retrieval set. In web-scale discovery systems, commonly available filters include those that restrict retrieval by material type and availability in the library collection.

FRBR (Functional Requirements for Bibliographic Records)—"An entity relationship model as a generalized view of the bibliographic universe, intended to be independent of any cataloging code or implementation" (Tillett 2004). FRBR is at the core of the new RDA description standards for cataloging. See also WEMI. More information is at http://www.loc.gov/cds/downloads/FRBR.PDF.

Full text—A full-text resource is one that provides access to the complete text of the works included. A full-text search is a search that looks for matches across the full-text of a document or resource.

Google Scholar—A subset of the Google search index, consisting of full-text journal articles, technical reports, preprints, theses, books, and other documents, including selected webpages that are of a scholarly nature. It includes full-text content from many major publishers and open-source content from National Library of Medicine, OCLC WorldCat, and HathiTrust, among others.

Harvest—"Method of extracting indexing and/or full text from remote web-accessible sites for the purpose of providing search and/or display from a central location" (NISO 2013).

HTML—"HTML is used to create the hypertext documents accessible via the World Wide Web and intranets, HTML script is a cross-platform presentation markup language that allows the author to incorporate into a Web page text, frames, graphics, audio, video, and links to other documents and applications" (Reitz 2014).

HTML 5—See HTML. HTML (version) 5 is capable of detecting and automatically adjusting to the device being used to access and display the code; thus, it is said to be "responsive" to various mobile platforms.

HTTP—"The communications protocol used to connect to Web servers on the Internet or on a local network (intranet). Its primary function is to establish a connection with the server and send HTML pages back to the user's browser" (*PC Magazine Encyclopedia* 2014).

Institutional Review Board (IRB)—IRBs approve proposed nonexempt research before involvement of human subjects may begin and are required by any institution accepting grant monies from the federal government. Most institutions involved in clinical research have standing IRBs that review all research projects involving human subjects associated with or sponsored by the institution. This frequently includes research done by libraries at these institutions, such as usability studies.

Integrated Library System (ILS)—An application, typically built on a relational database, that allows storage, creation, maintenance, search, and output of a library's bibliographic, acquisitions, serials control, patron, and circulation records. The ILS integrates all of these record types to create logical links among them, allowing library workers to build efficient workflows to manage resources.

IP range—"IP stands for Internet Protocol, the physical address of a client or server computer attached to a network governed by the TCP/IP protocol, written as four sets of Arabic numerals separated by dots (example: 123.456.78.9)" (Reitz 2014). An IP range is a range of IP addresses used by a particular institution for all the computers and devices on its network. IP ranges are commonly used by electronic subscription sources to restrict usage to users associated with a subscribing institution.

Keyword Searching—Searching that looks for a match in the parts of a bibliographic record included in the keyword index. This usually includes the title, abstract, and table of contents but also frequently includes the full body of the text for full-text items.

Lightweight Directory Access Protocol (LDAP)—"An application protocol for accessing and maintaining distributed directory information services over an Internet Protocol (IP) network" (Wikipedia 2014). LDAP is frequently used for "single sign-on" services, where a user logs in once with a password that is shared among several services. For example, the user logs into the library's catalog and the login is automatically passed to other library services requiring authentication.

Limiters—See Filters.

Link Resolver—Software that utilizes OpenURL standards and a knowledge base to connect a searcher from a citation to the actual object in the library or the electronic full-text content. If the content is subscribed to by the library, the link resolver will connect the searcher directly to it on the subscription content site. Common link resolver products include SFX, Metalib, and 360 Link.

Linked Data—"Linked data is a methodology for providing relationships between things (data, concepts and documents) anywhere on the web, using URI's for identifying, RDF for describing and HTTP for publishing these things and relationships, in a way that they can be interpreted and used by humans and software" (Koster 2009).

MARC—Literally, "machine-readable cataloging," MARC is a bibliographic data-encoding standard developed by the Library of Congress in the 1960s to store bibliographic metadata in machine-readable format. MARC 21, a major revision of MARC to unify the U.S. and Canadian standards, was released in 1999.

MARC tag—One of the data fields in MARC. The tag is the three-digit number associated with a particular field. For example, the title information is in the 245 tag, and the ISBN is in the 020.

MARC subfield—Most MARC tags (see definition above) have associated subfields that break out and codify further information stored in that field. For example, the 945 tag that includes holdings information about an item on some systems has a subfield a for call number data and a subfield g for copy number.

Metadata—Metadata is literally "data about data." Metadata usually refers to data describing an object in an encoded record of some type.

Metasearch—See Federated Search.

Multitenant—A system architecture in which a single instance of a software application serves multiple customers. Each customer is a "tenant."

Mutually Subscribed Content—Content for which the WSD service has a partnership agreement to provide full text and the library has a current subscription to the full text. Full text of this content can be searched and viewed directly (without an intervening link resolver) by authenticated searchers.

Open Access—"The free, immediate, availability on the public Internet of those works which scholars give to the world without expectation of payment—permitting any user to read, download, copy, distribute, print, search or link to the full text of these articles, crawl them for indexing, pass them as data to software or use them for any other lawful purpose" (SPARC 2014).

Open Archives Initiative–Protocol for Metadata Harvesting (OAI-PMH)—Developed by the Open Archives Initiative, OAI-PMH is a protocol to harvest the metadata of archival records. It is based on standard metadata included in the Dublin Core. More information is available at www.openarchives.org/pmh/.

OpenURL—A NISO standard that allows link resolvers to harvest data from bibliographic citations and send them in a URL request to content providers allowing automatic pass-through to full-text content.

OPAC (Online Public Access Catalog)—The expression first came into usage in the 1970s to describe computer-converted card catalogs with a public interface for searching by library users. Most OPACs are now HTML based and are accessed via a web browser.

OS (Operating System)—An operating system is the core software that controls a computer or device and manages all the programs (applications) installed on the machine. Common operating systems include Microsoft Windows, Linux, OS X for Macintosh, Android, and iOS.

Permalink—Short for permanent link, it is a stable URL to a source whose display link is dynamic. This allows users to capture a URL for a source that will not time out or change.

PHP—A programming language often used for web services applications and API. PHP is free software released under the PHP License.

Pipe—Another term for a connector in a federated search or metasearch application. See Connector.

Platform—"Originally referred to a specific type of computer hardware architecture, but the term now includes both the hardware and operating system installed on the CPU, usually for a model or entire family of computers (*examples*: Windows, Macintosh, UNIX)" (Reitz 2014).

Preharvested Index—"Metadata and full content systematically and periodically accumulated and processed in advance of searches; data is gathered from multiple sources and processed into a central index" (Hoeppner 2012).

Proxy Server—A server that comes between the workstation user and the Internet on an institution's private network. It provides security and administrative control and can also act as an authentication agent to outside services.

(Relevancy) Ranking Algorithm—"A ranking algorithm is the program used by a search engine to rank search results and display them in order of decreasing relevance based upon a set of pre-defined factors. While each search engine may assign different values to the various ranking factors, they usually consider the same factors overall" (NFAIS 2013).

RDA (Resource Description and Access)—A new description standard meant to replace and update AACR2 (Anglo American Cataloging Rules) adopted by national libraries in the United States, Canada, and several European countries. Records using the RDA standard went into general use in 2013. RDA is organized on the principles of FRBR and is hoped to be more compatible with the emerging discovery environment. More information is available at http://www.rdatoolkit.org.

RDF (Resource Description Framework)—A standard of the World Wide Web Consortium, it is a metadata data model based on the concept of the triple (subject-predicate-object). RDF is the data model used for linked data and is typically expressed in RDF/XML but has other serialization formats, including Turtle, N-Triple, and JSON-LD.

Reclamation—A service offered by OCLC to ensure that a library's holdings in WorldCat are accurately represented. It typically involves output of a library's catalog and other local records from the local integrated library system or other local database services in MARC format with a match point (usually OCLC number) that can be compared to the holdings currently on WorldCat.

RFP (Request for Proposals)—A formal bidding and selection process for acquisition of new products or services. RFPs are frequently required by government bodies or large institutions when purchasing critical and costly services or assets. RFPs bring structure to the purchasing process and ensure fairness in evaluation and selection of the winning bid. They define in detail the requirements of the purchasing body and help to limit risks by ensuring that the selected product/vendor can meet those requirements.

RSS—"Commonly referred to as 'Really Simple Syndication.' RSS is method of providing website content such as news stories or software updates in a standard XML format" (TechTerms.com 2014).

RUBY—An open-source programming language frequently used in API development and first released in the 1990s. It was heavily influenced by Perl, another commonly used Unix-based programming language.

Screen Scraping—"Simplest method of harvesting content that places no technical burden on the publishing site. The human readable text is extracted and indexed, formatted, and searched by various engines" (NISO 2013).

Search Engine—A program that searches the contents of documents. Web search engines specifically search documents, webpages, or data on the World Wide Web. Web search engines crawl and index the web and use proprietary relevancy-ranking algorithms to sort retrieval, bringing the most relevant results to the top. Popular web search engines include Google, Bing, and Yahoo.

Shibboleth—Open-source single sign-on software that is used by many higher education institutions in the United States.

Silo(ed)—"An application that does not interact with other applications or information systems. A siloed application is any software that functions on its own to solve a problem" (*PC Magazine Encyclopedia* 2014).

Single Sign-On (SSO)—An authentication process that allows users to sign in once with a single log-in and password and access many separate applications that require authentication.

SIP and SIP2—A protocol developed and controlled by 3M that has become a de facto standard for passing data from integrated library systems to self-service applications. SIP2 is version 2.0 of the standard.

SMS (Short Message Service)—The text-messaging communication used to transmit short messages between communications systems and devices, including mobile phones, fax machines, and IP addresses.

Social Media—Software and applications that allow people to interact with one another to create and share information. Social media grew out of the web-based technologies that characterize Web 2.0.

Web 2.0—The evolution of the web from static pages to pages that include technologies that allow users to interact with, add to, and change content.

Web-Scale Discovery (WSD)—"A pre-harvested central index coupled with a richly featured discovery layer that provides a single search across a library's local, open access, and subscription collections" (Hoeppner 2012).

Web Services—Web services provide data as a service using the http protocol. They allow programs to retrieve data direct from websites and use it in other applications.

WEMI—Literally, "work, entity, manifestation, item." WEMI is the entity model used by FRBR to describe different levels of bibliographic data. The work is the conceptual idea (e.g., Romeo and Juliet); the entity is how it is expressed (1968 Zefirelli film); the manifestation is the form (2000 DVD issued by Paramount); and the item is the physical expression (copy owned by the library).

WorldCat—The "online union catalog of materials cataloged by OCLC member libraries and institutions." More information is available at http://www.worldcat.org/whatis/default.jsp.

XML (eXtensible markup language)—A standardized markup language developed by the World Wide Web Consortium that describes a class of data objects and the behavior of computer programs that process them (NISO Metasearch Initiative 2006).

Z39.50—A client/server protocol for information retrieval from remote computers. The name refers to the standard that defines it: ANSI/NISO Z39.50 (NISO Metasearch Initiative 2006).

Glossary Sources

Hoeppner, Athena. 2012. "The Ins and Outs of Evaluating Web Scale Discovery Services." *Computers in Libraries* 32, no. 3: 7–10, 38–40.

Koster, Lukas. 2009. "Linked Data for Libraries." *CommonPlace.Net: Library 2.0 and Beyond*. http://commonplace.net/2009/06/linked-data-for-libraries.

NFAIS. 2013. *Recommended Practices: Discovery Services*. Philadelphia, PA: National Federation of Advanced Information Services. http://info.nfais.org/info/Recommended_Practices_Final_Aug_2013.pdf.

NISO Metasearch Initiative. 2006. "Metasearch XML Gateway Implementers Guide, Version 1.0." August 7. http://www.niso.org/publications/rp/RP-2006-02.pdf.

NISO Open Discovery Initiative Working Group. 2013. *Promoting Transparency in Discovery: A Recommended Practice of the National Information Standards Organization*. Baltimore, MD: NISO.

PC Magazine Encyclopedia. 2014. http://www.pcmag.com/encyclopedia/.

Reitz, Joan M. 2014. "ODLIS: Online Dictionary for Library and Information Science." http://www.abc-clio.com/ODLIS/odlis_f.aspx.

SPARC. 2014. "Why Open Access?" http://www.sparc.arl.org/resources/open-access/why-oa.

TechTerms.com. 2014. http://www.techterms.com/definition/rss.

Tillett, Barbara. 2004. "What Is FRBR? A Conceptual Model for the Bibliographic Universe." http://www.loc.gov/cds/downloads/FRBR.PDF

Unicode Consortium. 2014. "FAQ: Chinese and Japanese." http://www.unicode.org/faq/han_cjk.html.

Wikipedia. 2014. "Wikipedia: The Free English Encyclopedia." https://www.wikipedia.org.

Index

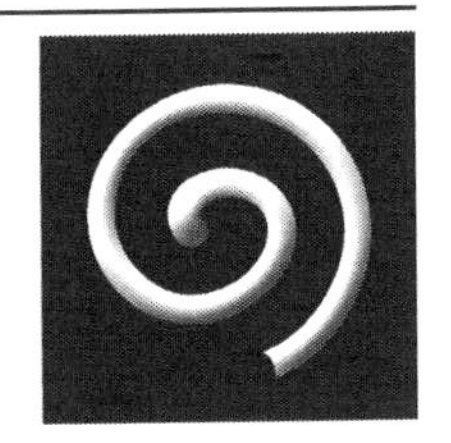

About the Author

JoLinda Thompson is technical systems coordinator at Himmelfarb Health Sciences Library and has more than fifteen years of experience as a library systems professional. In 2007 she began investigating next-generation OPACs and federated search systems and was a member of the committee that recommended the purchase of and then implemented the WebFeat federated search service for Himmelfarb. In 2010 she led a team charged with identifying and purchasing a web-scale discovery system to replace federated search. The two-year project culminated in release of EBSCO's Discovery Service to the library's users in fall 2012. She was lead author for a *Medical Reference Services Quarterly* article that details the process of purchasing and implementing EDS at Himmelfarb. She has a master in library science from the University of Pittsburgh and has been a senior member of the Academy of Health Information Professionals since 1993. She served as editor of *Technical Trends* for five years, the newsletter of the Technical Services Section of the Medical Library Association, and has numerous publications in the library literature.